# A Small World 2: Seek and Destroy

## Derek Jordan

*A Small World 2: Seek and Destroy* Copyright 2018 Derek Jordan

Publisher's Note:

This is a work of fiction. Any resemblance to actual persons-living or dead- references to real people, events, songs, business establishments or locales is purely coincidental. All characters are fictional, all events are imaginative.

978-0-9847775-7-0

Published by Jordan Marked Publishing
340 S Lemon Ave #6271
Walnut, California 91789


Author contact: djordan77@comcast.net

# Also by Derek Jordan

*Next of Kin*

*Drought (short story)*

*A Small World*

*Mammon (Coming soon)*

*Drought 2 (Coming soon)*

# Acknowledgements

To God, Nalani, Jaci, Speedy, Maribel, Anson, friends, the rest of my family, and supporters.

Special shout out to my editor Chris Ezzo. Appreciate the tools.

In loving memory of my father, Rudy C. Jordan.

## Prologue
## Dallas, Texas

The August evening was comfortable. Establishments had closed for the night, and people hurried home to relax and prepare for tomorrow's day of work. Earlier in the day, fog beclouded the sky after a flame-hot late morning. Bam felt that the current weather was compatible with his mood to strike. He wanted to finish his task, and end his eight-day stay in "The Lone Star State."

Bam leered through his binoculars long enough for Claude to cut two heads in his barbershop. Bam peeped the chatter and laughter in an establishment bought with Calvin's money. Calvin wanted Claude dead, and Bam couldn't wait until he could seize the moment. After two years of searching, Calvin had finally found out what state Claude resided in. Calvin was hell bent on revenge.

Calvin never forgot the horrid look on his wife's face when Claude and his team robbed him. He traveled from Florida to New Pine Grove cemetery in Waterbury, Connecticut to spit on Rocks's grave. Calvin thanked the heavens above that Link provided him the names of those responsible for his shattered pride before Link's sudden untimely death. Calvin conducted his business as usual, but the hunt for the ringleader and his followers became an obsession. With them dead, Calvin could breathe easily.

Bam brought himself back into Calvin's grace by locating Claude. Bam checked out an old victim of his on Facebook. He scrolled down J.Rock's friends list, landed on Jupe's page, clicked and enhanced a photo, and recognized Claude. Jupe was Claude's friend, and he was J-Rock's former co-worker. Jupe posted a photo when he traveled to Texas to attend a grand opening to a barbershop. Bam almost fainted when he saw a picture of Claude cutting the ribbon to signify the grand opening. *The motherfucker had the audacity to invest Calvin's money into something legit,* Bam thought. Bam hoped to end Claude's glory and prime with the bullets he had on him.

Bam was getting anxious. Bam hated the side of Claude's face. He wanted Claude in a plot. Even though Bam's boy Roscoe had a hand in the robbery, Bam overlooked Roscoe's betrayal and displaced his anger on Claude. Under normal circumstances, Calvin would have an employee tortured and killed for bringing a crook to the table. Still he spared Bam's life. Claude and his goons broke into Calvin's Southington home, robbed them at gunpoint, and walked away with cash, jewels, and Calvin's pride in a duffle bag. The mere thought if it made Bam grit his teeth.

Bam's hatred towards Claude turned into lust when a petite woman walked into the barbershop pushing a baby stroller, but his hatred returned when she walked up to Claude and gave him a kiss. With that in mind, Bam put the binoculars down and got out of the car. He dug into his breast pocket, and he pulled the photo of Claude cutting the ribbon to his barbershop. It was time for Claude to expire.

...

Claude Porter leaned in closely, and edged the hairline of a customer while a few of the locals threw jokes at his *James Harden* beard. Sonya playfully added her tidbit to the action. Claude held a smirk on his face.

"Lets not talk about that *Carlos Boozer* hairline of yours. Homeboy went to *Staples* and got his shit done with a *Sharpie*," Claude said jokingly.

The occupants bent over in laughter, including Claude's customer sitting in the chair. The patrons roared with excitement and laughter as Claude continued to rank on the local. Sonya smiled, sat down with their daughter Jasmin, and shook her head while watching Claude continue to trade jokes.

The last two years had been fruitful. A few days after Claude made Dallas, Texas his permanent address, Jasmin was conceived. Claude and Sonya were married a few months after Mark and Fatima tied the knot, who also had a son born two days before Jasmin. Everyone was happy, but Sonya knew Claude's past actions in Connecticut haunted him. This much was true, but she was still unaware of the bodies he dropped. Claude was cagey. He always looked over his shoulder. They quarreled because of the guns Claude kept in the condo. She would urge him to seek help, but he had to maintain the darkest secret he'd every carried. Claude chose to live in denial. As a couple, Claude and Sonya were fine and happy. Still, like any relationship, there was a hint of darkness. The goons Claude gunned down mentally scarred him, but he'd do it again if he had to.

As the men continued to laugh and bullshit, Sonya thought about her own drama that she'd brought to the table. Morbid memories of Aaron crossed her mind. She felt guilt surrounding his murder. She fought that memory by reminding herself of the stalking, beatings, and the rape by Aaron's hand.

Trudy crossed her mind every day. Her death

was the main reason Sonya sought therapy. After all, Trudy's death hit her like a ton of bricks. Sonya blamed herself for her friend's murder because of her close association with Flex. Sonya regretted not going to the funeral. It weighed on her mind. Sonya gave Trudy a grave warning the last time they conversed. Sonya remembered dialing Trudy's number repeatedly, and getting no answer. And a few weeks later, after Sonya suffered another assault from the hands of Aaron, a detective told her that Trudy's decomposing corpse was found, and that Flex confessed to murdering her.

An hour later, after the last customer stepped out of the barbershop, the two other barbers followed him, leaving Claude and his family alone.

"Baby, you didn't have to wait for me. I know you're tired," Claude said.

Jasmin walked to him with her arms opened, beckoning her father to pick her up. Claude snatched her off the ground, and he benched pressed her. Sonya approached him with her own greeting. Sonya hugged Claude and the baby and kissed them.

"I'll never leave you baby. I love you," Sonya said.

"I love you too," Claude stated. "I just want you

to take care of yourself."

Sonya had an urge to tell him he should be caring for himself, however, if she spoke up, an argument would be inevitable. Claude wasn't a fan of being told that he needed therapy.

"I know baby," she said dismissively.

Claude knew what she was thinking. Deciding to move forward, he switched the subject.

"We have to stop at the store and pick up some shit for Mark. He has been hounding me all day, but I do want to eat. His ribs be on point."

Sonya smiled. "I've been craving those ribs all day baby. Fatima just texted me to remind you."

Claude and Sonya exchanged more small talk before walking out of the door. Claude locked it behind him, looked left and right, and continued across the street towards a crowded lot in which he parked his car. He spotted a familiar face lingering amongst the Texans. Claude didn't keep eye contact with him. Claude knew exactly who the freckled man was, but he didn't have time to invest any thought into it. It could only mean one thing; Calvin knew where he was. He walked Sonya and Jasmin to the car before telling her he'd forgotten something in the shop. Claude knew he'd been spotted, and he needed a quick solution to separate his family. He prepared for the Grim Reaper's arrival since he and the others robbed the capo. Claude was ready to face his past.

"Can't you get it tomorrow baby? We need to get going. Jasmin is tired and hasn't eaten yet."

Claude said, "Its my business phone. I need it. Be right back."

Before Sonya had a chance to speak, Claude was already walking toward the barbershop with a heart full of murder. When he unlocked the door, he walked inside and left the door ajar.

...

Bam waited for a group of rowdy teens to walk by before manually cocking his weapon. Bam knew he'd caught Claude slipping. Bam was so anxious that he almost dropped his gun. He placed a smirk on his face, and was on his way to making Calvin a happy man. He pushed the door open expecting to see Claude's back, but Claude was nowhere in sight. It caught Bam off guard. Bam walked slowly through the barbershop with his gun trained. He moved with caution until he reached the backroom. Bam's paranoia was heightened. If Claude walked in seconds before him, then where the fuck was he? Bam turned around and walked to the only spot Claude could be.

Bam opened the bathroom door and saw no sign of Claude, but Bam felt Claude's presence behind the door at the last second before Claude rammed the blade into Bam's face. Claude shoved the blade so deep that he had trouble pulling it out. Bam recoiled in blistering pain. He stabbed him repeatedly with powerful thrusts until Bam's body stopped moving. Blood spewed everywhere. Claude's face and clothes were covered in it. Claude panted and breathed heavily over the corpse. On cue, Claude's cell phone rang.

"Sonya, take the car and bring Jasmin home. I'll catch up with you later," Claude said gravely.

"Claude, what's wrong? I don't like how you sound and your scaring me," Sonya said.

Claude knew she wasn't going to leave quietly. He blew a huge sigh as he stared at the body he carved out, but Claude prepped her with a code that never should be questioned.

"Karma."

"Wh...what?" Sonya was in shock.

Claude said, "Sonya, please!! I don't want to yell at you! This is some real shit! Go! Get Jasmin out of here! I'm ok! Go!"

When Sonya hung up, Claude called Mark.

...

Mark weaved in and out of traffic with perspiration dripping down his face. Mark loved the life he was living, but Claude told him the money he robbed could later come with a hefty price. Mark thought about Fatima and their child. The thought of anything happening to them made Mark nauseas.

When he pulled up in front of the store, Mark took a deep breath and stepped out of the car. He prepared for the worst.

# 1

## Jamaica City, Texas

Calvin King clinked his champagne glass with his wife, Jessica, and the blue eyed brunette real estate agent after closing out on a beachfront home. The threesome sipped from their glasses and celebrated inside to avoid the chilly weather. Calvin was excited by the smile Jessica had on her face. It hadn't left since Calvin accepted the terms of the agreement. He knew she liked the sounds of the sea and the sight of it at night. The beachfront house was the best gift Jessica ever received.

Calvin made Jessica a promise that he'd make up for the home invasion. The frightening event took a toll on her mental status. First came therapy, and the meds soon after. The incident fueled Calvin's desire to kill every single motherfucker responsible.

After the robbery, it was business as usual. Calvin's cash flow amplified tenfold, and he never assembled a thought of stopping. Despite his success in the underworld, memories of the black masked men picked at his pride. Glum thoughts of lining the bandits up against the wall and opening fire with an assault rifle made his penis hard. Calvin would stare at Claude's photo and create images of gunning him down.

Three weeks ago, Bam told him some good news about Claude's whereabouts. He was so excited about Bam finding Claude on *Facebook* that he bought Jessica a Maybach. Calvin rarely smiled, but it spread across his ugly black face. When Calvin smiled, so did everyone else because he rarely did. Calvin wore the smile until the present day.

"Mr. King, you made the perfect purchase. When you rise in the morning, rain or shine, the sea will greet you," the energetic real estate agent said. She looked at Jessica and her beauty, and she took a good look at Calvin. The real estate agent found Calvin monstrous, but his greenbacks were attractive. The real estate agent knew Calvin had to be a kingpin to possess that kind of woman and wealth.

Calvin wrapped his beefy arm around Jessica. "I'm not too crazy about the water, especially when there is a motherfuckin' hurricane coming, but the Mrs. is dying to decorate in here. Not one of the best properties I bought, but Jessica thinks so," Calvin said with a hint of arrogance. He kissed his wife softly on the lips.

Calvin's phone buzzed in his pocket. He'd been waiting for Bam's call for confirmation of Claude's death. He excused himself from the women and stepped out onto the deck overlooking the Gulf of Mexico. He pulled his phone out of his pocket and answered it.

"What's the word Bam?" Calvin asked.

"That I'm going to kill you," Claude threatened with a hushed tone.

"Bam, I don't got time for these goddamn games man. Is the job done or what?" Calvin was losing his patience.

Claude said, "Me either. And no, the job isn't done. In the meantime, check your text message and you let me know if I'm playing games." The phone disconnected.

Calvin walked out of the women's view, and he received the text. When he checked it, he saw a gruesome image of Bam's gutted face and neck. Calvin was flabbergasted. Calvin called Bam's phone again, and it went straight to voicemail. Calvin looked at his phone long and hard, and he knew Bam met his match. Bam's phone was in his adversary's possession. Memories of the frightened look on his wife's face while she held their newborn daughter rushed his brain. Calvin walked back into the view of the women, and turned his back to them. The sea provided him with a little tranquility, but he knew what he was capable of. Calvin was a businessman, but he killed on the way up to the top. He wasn't afraid of Claude, but he had to respect him. Bam knew where Claude worked, ate, and shat, but Calvin didn't. And with Bam's phone in Claude's possession, Claude now had the upper hand. The only silver lining in Calvin's case was that Bam's phone was a disposable burner phone.

Calvin didn't waste any more time thinking about the matter. He wrapped up the small celebration, parted ways with the real estate agent, and headed back on the highway. Bam was replaceable, and he never found it in his heart to grieve for an employee. With Bam gone, he knew just the person that would replace him.

...

The Los Angeles sky was gray, and it promised heavy rain. It had been piping-hot all week, and the cemetery Simone's body rested in needed the relief. Ali hovered over her grave in silence. He didn't have a lot of time left. Police caught wind of where he had been hiding the last few years, but he found out first and took on the road. Broke and out of options, Ali accepted an old friend's proposal, and was headed to

New York.

Ali had to pay a few visits before hitting the road. A half hour earlier, he watched a growing Khalif from a distance for ten minutes. The family forbade Ali from seeing him because they knew his actions got Simone killed. They knew he had a hand in her killer's murder, but her family was God-fearing. They believed vengeance was with the Lord; Ali had no right avenging Simone's murder. After realizing he would never see Khalif again because of a murder warrant, Ali leaked a few tears before heading out of the cemetery. Ali had no regret though. In reality, Flip was actually Aaron's murderer, but the gun Flip used to kill Aaron belonged to Ali. Ali used the same gun on a crack head he had killed over a twenty dollar debt. Ballistics proved the bullet shells from both crime scenes matched, and the police were on Ali's ass. Ali understood the murder warrant, and he would never rat Flip out. Ali would rather blow his own head off than to betray his cousin. Besides, after Flip fired his one and only lethal shot, Ali dumped the rest of the magazine into Aaron's corpse.

Ali was getting tired. He was tired of being on the run. Relocating across North America was ideal. He hated his situation, but he had no regret. Rage would flood his brain whenever Ali thought about the night he found Simone's slain corpse. He had planned a life with her and their son. In hindsight, Ali had multiple chances of killing Aaron for killing his cousin Colin. It wasn't part of the plan. Ali's intention was to kill Aaron, and to take back what he felt was rightfully his, but Simone caught the deadly end of the stick. Ali felt responsible.

The last memory Ali had of Wade was the night of the massacre. An hour after parting with him, Wade's body was shot and burned beyond recognition. Ali skipped town two days before Wade's family, including Noemi, dispersed Wade's ashes in the Pacific Ocean. Two of the closest people he had in his orbit were gunned down in the same night. Aaron deserved every piece of bullet that pierced through his body.

Ali kissed Simone's tombstone one final time before walking away from it. He had thousands of miles to cover before starting a new, dark phase of his life. Perhaps a phase that could lead him to hell.

## 2

## Fort Worth, Texas

The temperature dropped a few degrees since Claude stuck a cold sharp blade into Bam's face. The chilly weather and nightfall was on Claude and Mark's side as they scanned for lookers, and a spot to dump the cadaver. When Claude saw it, Mark looked around the area for breaches. They found none. Bam's body was wrapped up like a brand new memory foam mattress. It was covered with a black, old oilcloth, and secured at the legs with a twenty-five pound chain to ensure Bam's deposit into the lake. Claude and Mark pulled and tugged the corpse out the trunk of the SUV. On the count of three, they tossed the body into the water. It didn't take long for the body to hit the floor of the lake.

...

Five days after leaving Los Angeles, Ali was a few blocks away from Raven's apartment in Brooklyn, New York. Anxiety swamped him as he drove through the heavy and annoying traffic. The proposal she laid on him was righteous for his situation. All she needed was protection, but Ali viewed Raven as a deserter and coward. Ali couldn't turn down the money despite Raven discharging herself in the middle of a war with

Aaron and Flex.

It was a long drive. Ali spent five days in the car with his morbid memories. The memory of Simone's opened eye corpse stretched out in their bed jolted him out of daydreams while driving. He thought of his bane life. At that point, Ali secretly embraced death. He didn't know what he was getting into fucking with Raven, but he depleted all of his options. Every day, Ali felt he was getting close to his expiration date. He felt like a wounded dog running away from home preparing to die. He did too much dirt to live a quiet life. Society wanted him in a plot or cage. Ali vowed that no law enforcement would take him alive.

It was his first time visiting the big apple. At every traffic light, Ali scanned the people and the buildings. He was used to the big city, but New York carried a different aura and demeanor. Ali liked it and wondered if he could live out his years in New York peacefully. Not one to increase his own hope, he tossed the thought from his mind, and continued his journey to his destination.

Ali parked the car three streets away from Raven's apartment, and had to walk with his GPS in his hand. It was eighty degrees, and he only had a duffle bag that contained as follows: three outfits, some weed, toiletries, and a loaded pistol. He walked past a diversity of people before reaching the staircase of Raven's brownstone. Ali took two steps up the staircase before Raven walked outside to greet him. The second Ali laid eyes on her, he skipped a breath. He almost forgot about the homicidal thoughts he harbored of her. Raven resembled a model on the cover of *Vanity Fair*. Her beauty was surreal and serene, but underneath her exterior, she had the heart of a villain. Ali stopped in his tracks and met Raven's hazel eyes. He walked up the stairs slowly, diverted his eyes off her body, and walked right past her into her home. Raven sighed and prepared for a clash. The tension was too thick to avoid.

# 3

## Coral Harbour

The blue sea provided tranquility to those who sought it. The white sand covered a portion of paradise. Residents and tourists flooded the area, relieved to spend some time away from their stressful lives. It was a perfect getaway. When social strain hits home, Coral Harbour was where one could go to get away from it all. It consisted of miles of unspoiled beach, peaceful mangroves, and a myriad of tropical flora. Claude bought the Bahamian style residence for the family after he flipped the blood money a few times, and through multiple properties being rented for big money. Every room in the home had an ocean view. The home reflected the elegance of Bahamian Colonial style with high ceilings.

Claude, Mark, Sonya, Fatima, and Sahara sat in the living room as if they were on their way to a funeral. Claude and Mark just flew in an hour ago, and they were waiting for Claude to speak. It was the perfect time. Destiny, Jasmin, and Meadow were in the next room asleep. Sonya and Fatima were still unaware of their reasoning for being taken to paradise. The women and children arrived hours after Claude's *incident*. They found it hopeless to question the men about what was going on, but they knew it had to be serious for Claude to abruptly pull them away from their lives. The women were anxious, uncertain, and pissed that the men weren't talking.

"Somebody tried to assassinate me last night, but it went south for him," Claude said quietly.

Claude's revelation made everyone speechless, excluding Mark. Claude's demeanor spelled murder. Claude told Sahara last night in full detail when he picked her up from her condo. She was forbidden to reveal it. Sonya and Fatima's fear was indescribable, but they had to know. Everyone digested the news without saying a word.

"So where is the body?" Fatima asked. Terror flashed in her eyes.

"Not relevant," Mark answered.

"Why is it not relevant Mark? He told us everything else. We were better off not knowing. Now we are all suffering from *his* fucked up past," Fatima said without thinking. It got Sahara's attention, and she didn't like how Fatima's statement oozed out of her mouth.

"Fatima, now is not the time for your extra shit. You living off of C's bloody money just like the rest of us. How dare you insult my brother after everything he had done for you!" Sahara quipped.

The tension got fat. Claude leaned calmly against the wall. Mark tried to intervene, but he was cut short by Fatima.

Fatima looked at her sister. "I think it is the time Sonya! Somebody tried to kill your husband because of his past. God knows how many bodies he dropped after *that* revelation. He relocated our lives and our children. Someone could have followed us down here. Our children don't deserve this shit. We need..."

"Fatima!" Mark blasted. Claude continued to smoke on the roach clip before putting it out.

"Yeah Fatima, you need to chill with all that ungrateful shit. I feel you on the move down here, but talking shit ain't going to get us out of this situation," Sahara said. Sahara didn't like Fatima's rant. She couldn't believe her audacity. If Mark weren't her husband, she would have jabbed her.

"Fatima, real talk, don't say nothing else! You out of line right now, and I'm a little embarrassed," Mark said thickly.

Claude said, "Don't be Mark. It's all good and she has a right to be mad, but I tell you one thing Fatima; all this fine living came with a price. My bad for the inconvenience, but I'm doing my best to keep y'all safe and to make this arrangement as comfortable as possible."

Fatima looked around incredulously.

"Comfortable? Really Claude? I don't think someone that reappeared from your past coming to kill you is comfortable. And who knows what happened in Connecticut for that person to come after you." Fatima was so livid that she didn't realize she crossed the line.

"Mark, tell your wife something. She's out of control," Sahara said calmly despite the rage that came upon her. Sahara knew what Claude did, but blood ties only held that secret. Sahara never had a problem with Fatima until now.

They debated and argued about being taken away from their situated lives until sunset. The drama cooled down, but the tension between Sahara and Fatima remained.

...

It was seven in the morning. Claude watched Sonya sleep while she lay naked over the comforter. He got an arousal looking at her. Claude loved her, and would die for her. He wasn't planning to die or allow his family to succumb to the hands of Calvin, but the pieces to the puzzle were scattered. With that in mind, he put on some jogging pants, a wife beater, and sneakers. After getting dressed, Claude kissed Sonya on her forehead, retrieved the .22 from the lockbox, and walked out of the front door en route to the beach.

The sound of the sea was a remedy for the turmoil that flooded Claude's mind. The noise in his head was loud, and he couldn't focus on a plan because he didn't have one.

A few beach bums stepped into his vision as he gawked at the ocean. Something had to give, but he cringed at the thought of going back to prison. Claude knew he had to kill Calvin, but how would he get near him? Calvin was a boss among bosses, and he always had suited men with loaded guns nearby. Calvin was a stone cold killer and he was creative, but he was human. Nonetheless, Claude was determined.

# 4

## Webster CI

## Cheshire, CT

Inmates shared war stories and discharge planning. Correction officers spoke of overtime, years of service, unruly inmates, and their personal lives. It was a typical morning in the level two prison, but Tank had only a few days left in the shit hole. They'd be the longest two to four days of his life.

Tank's anxiety increased tenfold as the tension mounted in the streets. He'd been off them a month after Claude was discharged, and it had been quiet. Tank had blood money stashed away, and he passed up on a work release program five months ago so he could serve out the rest of his time. The work release program, Tank figured, would only set him back on his mission, and make him a sitting duck for anyone trying to end him. Calvin King had big number figures on those responsible for strong-arming him. Tank knew Calvin wouldn't rest until he killed them all.

Tank made many desperate attempts to reach his crew, but was unsuccessful. He was writing Claude a warning letter about Chester creating buzz in the street about Claude knocking off his uncle Link, Domino, Twalique and Ty. Tank tried to reach him.

Claude's phone kept going to voicemail. The talk grew more powerful than a snowball going down hill. Silencing Chester was in question, and Tank would gladly eliminate him from any equation.

After sealing the letter, Tank laid on his bunk bothered by uncertainty. He tried to reach Zane on numerous occasions, but was unable to contact her. Zane was good for her disappearing acts. The timing was fucked up, and her life was in grave danger.

...

Passengers walked off the Metro North train station in herds. Some were coming from other towns in Connecticut. Most of them were coming from Grand Central Station in New York City. Locals, businessmen, and hoodlums walked down the steps of the platform, and onto Meadow Street in Waterbury, Connecticut where they hopped into waiting vehicles and taxis.

A tall stout Hispanic man was the last passenger to get off the train. His gaze was sharp. A shroud of stubble obscured his jaw. He had a half-inch scar on the side of his neck. His long, black hair was tied into a braid, and it touched the small of his back. He carried an army-sized duffle bag. Inside of it, two days of clothing concealed two silencers, three knives, and ammunition. The man was evil, deadly, and prepared to make loved ones weep. He walked straight to a decked out, tinted black Denali. After putting his bag in the trunk, he got inside, and the driver pulled off.

...

Three hours later, Tommy slept soundly in the *Super Eight* motel. He had an action packed bout of unprotected sex, and he was worn out. Life had been lavish for him. Tommy's days consisted of weed, blowing money in chunks, and widespread whoring. After doing a three-month bid, Tommy created a grand entrance into a swank lifestyle. If he had an accountant, Tommy would have been told that his stint as a playboy was coming to an abrupt end. The blood money he risked his life for came and went like an illusion. Tommy was two days away from finding out the most devastating news he ever heard...that he was back to being broke.

Tommy opened his eyes from his deep somber, and he almost forgot where he was. He had plenty of those kinds of nights, and it wasn't anything new. Tommy dipped his nose in many piles of cocaine, and he felt like he was literally on top of the world.

Tommy wore a face of confusion when he realized he was soaked. He thought that maybe he or the bitch he jumped off with pissed the bed, but the texture was thicker than urine. He turned on the lamp next to the bed. His eyes were wild with fear. The blond, blue-eyed skank he courted and fucked lay motionless on the bed, blood gushing from her neck. Tommy recoiled from the body and landed on the floor. A six foot five Latin killer obstructed his view of the ceiling. The shine of his two-inch blade sparkled in his left hand. He kicked Tommy in his midsection. Tommy curled into a fetal position from the excruciating blow. The pain was unbearable. The lone figure kneeled, grabbed Tommy by the back of his neck, inched his face near Tommy's ear, and pressed the knife on his neck.

The Latin man whispered, "You're just as guilty, but we're willing to give you a pass if you tell me where the girl is."

Tommy had no options because of the knife pressed against his jugular, and the indescribable pain he was in. Without warning, Tommy spat a ball of phlegm in the man's face. The man cracked a smile after removing Tommy's debris off of it.

"So its death before dishonor for you, huh? That takes the fun out of it. I hope Tank and Zane live it up just like you did...because their days are numbered...

just like your ringleader amigo. He may kill Bam, but he no kill me. Calvin and Chester send condolences," the man said coldly.

The Latin killer removed the blade from Tommy's neck and gutted his body. The killer poked and twisted the knife in him until Tommy stopped moving. The man stood up over his new kill and marveled at his work. Tommy's face and body looked mangled. Blood pooled around his face and body. After wiping the blade that killed over a dozen people, the man walked out the sleazy motel like nothing happened. The man got back into the same black Denali that brought him to the motel. Claude, Tank, and Zane were MIA, but the murderer vowed to find them soon.

# 5

## Brooklyn, NY

African art, sculptures, and family photos adorned the living room walls. Raven barely watched the sixty-inch smart TV because of her business in the underworld, but she wanted it. It made her brownstone apartment look swank. The tension in it was thick though. Two days drifted since Ali's arrival. He slept the majority of the time, but throughout the last twenty minutes, their words towards one another were thick and filled with malice. They sat across from one another with anxiety drenched on their faces. Ali was stewed, and he could barely keep his composure. Raven was nervous, but Ali was oblivious to the .22 she stashed before he woke up. Ali was unpredictable and posed a threat. Raven wasn't taking any chances.

"So that's what you think of me? A coward because I didn't want to see anymore death?" Raven asked.

Raven was pissed, but she knew Ali was going to bash her for leaving Los Angeles.

"I know you a coward. Fuckin' excuses. And you want to show a nigga mercy after he pulled the plug on your brother. That's real civil," Ali said thickly.

Raven said, "Fuck you Ali! Since you want to

throw shit back in my face, don't act like you and Wade weren't crawling around like scavengers. Y'all would've been still nickel and diming if it weren't for me putting y'all onto some real money. I bet you Simone was relieved that your broke ass was bankin' major money because of me. You couldn't stand on your own two feet, never mind your family."

Raven opened her mouth to say one more word, but Ali cut it short when he stood up steeped with anger. The truth stung him in the gut. Raven reacted quickly, and she drew her weapon. Ali ceased his movement.

"Bitch, you don't got the heart. Now use it before you give me a chance to come for your throat," Ali said icily.

Raven's hand shook as she held the gun. She knew it was worthless pulling a gun out on someone who was wanted for murder. Ali's eyes were wide and intense and his body language spelled no fear. She put the gun down, sat on the couch, and got a hold of herself. He took a deep breath to calm himself.

"Don't ever do that shit again," Ali said, still fuming.

Fifteen minutes passed before Raven broke the ice.

"Can we please come to our senses? Can I tell you the reason why I sought you out?" she asked. Ali pursed his lips and looked at her.

"A guy named Percy Wetmore ran over my mother and killed her. I want him dead. Lorenzo Boyd robbed me after my boyfriend was killed seven months ago. I have no protection. I need your help, and that's the extent of it." Raven left the living room, came back with a manila envelope, and placed it in from of him. Ali was still salty from their clash, but he knew he had to put it behind him. Ali pulled the photos out of the envelope, studied their faces and the package's descriptive contents, and placed the material back into the envelope.

Ali saw the fear in Raven's eyes. He still thought she had a lot of nerve with that proposal shit knowing that Raven ran because of the growing violence. Ali took that retreat shit seriously. Ali would have murdered Wade if he'd pulled some coward shit like that. A few minutes ago, Raven smeared Simone in his face like a pile of feces. Ali would have killed anyone else for saying that. He was angry and prideful, but Ali couldn't find it in his cold heart to turn his back on her. Despite the circumstances, they had history.

During the rest of the conversation, Ali learned

that Raven found him through Noemi, Wade's former fiancé. Raven explained to Ali that Noemi told her everything about the murders, including Aaron being shot to death on Raven's bedroom floor. The thought of Aaron coming to kill her haunted her.

Ali listened attentively as Raven described both men in detail.

# 6

## Coral Harbour

Sonya was on her cell phone thanking her friend Nicole for stopping by the condo in Dallas, and retrieving the mail that accumulated within the last two weeks. Claude fingered through every piece of it until he saw the letter Tank wrote him. Claude opened it, read the contents, and walked away from Sonya's wondering eyes. She excused herself from their conversation and followed him.

Claude's phone vibrated while he pondered the letter. Sonya appeared and stood in the doorway. Claude remained silent as he listened to the caller. His body language revealed bad news from the caller, and from the letter Tank sent him. Sonya's curiosity peaked. When Claude ended the call and finished the letter, Sonya walked into the room. She cared less about her own intrusiveness, but she knew her husband; it looked like someone flipped his world upside down. She held Claude tight despite being oblivious to the news someone dropped on him.

"Baby, what's wrong?" Sonya asked softly.

Claude was in shock. The letter never left his hand. He studied her eyes and found nothing but warmth. The news of Tommy's death hit him hard, and he fought hard to keep the tears from falling from his eyes.

"Nothing baby. Just some bullshit drama popping off back home. Nothing for you to worry about," he said casually. He diverted his eyes off of hers, and he walked out the room. Sonya watched Claude's back while he walked, and she knew he was hiding something.

After hearing the back door close, Sonya looked out the window and saw Claude approach Mark, who stood casually, while he flipped steaks on the grill. Fatima laid in the sun, and the kids sat together playing with toys. Sonya watched Claude like a hawk. He pulled Mark away from the grill. Claude spoke to him in private, and Mark walked back to the grill as if the conversation wasn't a big deal. Sonya fought the urge to walk outside and confront him about the letter and phone call, but she decided against it. Sonya thought better to go outside to try to enjoy the rest of the evening with the family.

...

The next morning, Sonya woke up alone. Claude wasn't at her side. She walked into the living room where Mark was, and she decided to probe him.

"Good morning. C running on the beach early,

huh?" Sonya asked.

Mark was in a funk. He was watching the television. He wasn't paying attention to what was on. He was thinking hard. The stressed look on Mark's face betrayed him. Sonya knew something was wrong. Sonya had a feeling it had something to do with the letter and phone call Claude received yesterday.

"He ain't running on the beach. He's gone Sonya," Mark said flatly.

"What do you mean he is gone, Mark? What the fuck is going on?" Her southern drawl was thick, and her tone was elevated. She rarely swore. The secrecy was taking a toll on her.

Mark looked at her and buried his head back into the safety net of his arms.

"Connecticut." He took a deep breath.

"Wha...why?" Sonya felt like a spell of dizziness was creeping upon her. She took a seat. She allowed the news Mark dropped on her to sink in. She felt exposed and vulnerable without Claude being by her side.

"The letter, phone call? Is that why he left?" Tears spilled down her face.

"Yeah."

Sonya asked, "Mark, what's going on? I don't

care about all that 'he's protecting you bullshit.' He's your cousin, but he's my husband, and I have a right to know."

"Tommy is dead, that's what's going on," Mark said dryly.

Sonya only heard of Tommy, but she had never seen the man. She understood Claude lost another one of his best friends, but she didn't want to lose her family based on Claude's disappearance. Sonya felt that the family was a higher priority. She heard countless Rocks and Tommy stories, and it wasn't a surprise.

"So he brings us here, and now he leaves again. Who's he protecting? Us or his friends?" Sonya asked loudly.

Mark knew she was hurting. Sonya's comment was insensitive. She was getting more distraught by the second. Mark deemed it a natural reaction.

"Look Sonya, this entire situation is fucked up, but you have to trust him right now," Mark said patiently.

"Mark, is Tommy's death related to what we are going through right now?"

"I honestly don't know Sonya, but I tell you one thing; it either has something to do of what we are all

Derek Jordan

going through, or it could be related to what he is not telling you," Mark said.

"Mark, please," Sonya said, her tears falling freely down her face. "Why is he keeping me in the dark? That's the problem. He's fuckin' paranoid, he keeps a gun inside of his junk drawer, he rarely goes out with me anymore, and when he does, he has a gun on him. He doesn't tell me anything! He didn't even have the decency to tell me that he was leaving!"

Sonya lost it. She wept loudly. Mark placed her in his arms telling her that everything was going to be all right.

"Listen to me Sonya. I am not at liberty to discuss what he is not telling you. You are right; Claude is a fucking wreck, and he should be. He knows he is failing you, which is why he felt that it is time to face his monster. He's tired Sonya, and he wants his family alive. The shit that he ain't telling you is real as fuck. This is shit that he can't even tell a therapist. Am I aware of what he went through? Absolutely. That is something he is going to take to his grave. It is pointless to press him about it because he ain't telling you. Me and C spoke about that shit once, and I never heard anything about it again. Let that man be Sonya. He loves you more than life itself, and

42

he is doing what a man is supposed to do. He is trying to protect his family and you have to accept that. And if he doesn't do anything about it, we are ALL dead!"

The silence between them was thick. Mark's words hit her like a ton of bricks. She knew something morbid went down with her husband a few years ago. It would be naïve to think that he never killed anyone.

"Where is everyone?" Sonya asked. Her eyes had a haunted look, and they swam with tears.

"Sahara and Fatima took the kids out to the beach."

"With no protection Mark?"

"Dino flew in this morning. He is watching them," Mark said.

Without saying another word, she left Mark standing in the middle of the living room. Mark knew that Claude was entering the beginning phases of a horrific storm.

# 7

## New York

Lorenzo Boyd finished a glamorous night of popping bottles, and mingling with the upper class. The diamond crucifix around his neck glistened as he casually bopped out of the gentlemen's club on W 45$^{th}$ Street. Lorenzo stood over six feet tall, and had the build of a track star. He was cocky, boisterous, and dangerous. Lorenzo was twenty-four, and he was already a veteran in the prison system. Lorenzo had no skill, but enough rip and run money to start a business.

The target Lorenzo scoped all night looked like he was sitting on some serious paper. Lorenzo had no intention of robbing anyone tonight, but the short thin dude he stalked rocked the bling. Lorenzo was drawn to the shine, and he wanted it. He told his cronies that he would link up with them later. Lorenzo wanted the big fish all to himself. The rings on the man's fingers shone like the link around his neck. The dude looked like a lame wearing bling, and he was easy picking.

Lorenzo started the engine of his 2014 BMW i8 Coupe, pulled away from the curb, and trailed the vic. A grin of greed etched on his face while he followed the decked out dark blue Lexus. In reality, Lorenzo was good with money. He was comfortable, but Lorenzo knew the blood money wouldn't get longer if he didn't work for it. He'd spent countless hours studying his targets. Lorenzo risked his life numerous times so he could push fast cars and live glamorously.

The lame stepped out of his car on $52^{nd}$ and went inside a small nightclub. Lorenzo followed him inside. He watched his mark for two hours before following him to a four-bedroom house in the suburbs in Jamaica Estates. Lorenzo never traveled the area, but the neighborhood was upper class. He planned on returning to it for an easy take.

Lorenzo stopped and killed the engine four houses down from where the target parked. He had no more plans for the night, so he planned on staking the dude out. He lit a Newport, inhaled it, and exhaled out the driver's side window. Lorenzo felt no guilt for what he was about to do, for he justified his actions by taking what someone can make back. Lorenzo was the shit, and he knew it. People hated, feared, and respected him. Lorenzo valued that over money, and he was willing to die for both.

Lorenzo spotted no activity in the neighborhood. While screwing on the suppressor of his gun, his Galaxy phone vibrated. It was the freak bitch he met last week and fucked outside in the back of a nightclub. He pondered the idea of taking her to his bed so he could have more flexibility with her. He masturbated during the week with the image of the session. Ignoring his own cardinal rule of being distracted while on a job, he answered the phone.

"So you decided to call me. What you like to drink ma?" Lorenzo asked with a smirk on his face.

The woman chuckled seductively. "Oh shit, it's like that baby? You fittin' to treat me like a queen tonight?"

"You already know. I want to hear you call me daddy when I wrap those legs around my shoulders," Lorenzo countered. He made no plans on spending money on a thot that he fucked amidst grime and trash, but she was going to smoke his weed, sniff his coke, and drink his liquor. That would serve as compensation for the suck and fuck.

"I want to call you daddy baby. I want to suck that big dick of yours, and my pussy has been screaming for it. So what time should I expect to get fucked?" she asked bluntly.

Lorenzo said, "It's eleven now so I say maybe between two or three. I know it will be late and all that shit, but will you wait for your king?"

"Ill wait a decade for that king dick of yours baby," she said.

The smile on Lorenzo's face disappeared when he saw his target coming towards the driver's side door through the mirror. Lorenzo managed to get a hold of his gun, but the lame was quicker. He already had his hand in the window. Lorenzo's target used his long blade like it was a part of his hand and swiped it two inches deep in Lorenzo's neck. Blood spilled from it profusely. The whore on the phone said hello a few times before hanging up. He watched Lorenzo make a feeble attempt to stop the bleeding from his neck, but it was useless. The target watched him suffer before he stopped moving for good.

Ali looted the body and car before escaping back to the city. Killing Lorenzo was a lot easier than he thought. Ali had no problem enticing the stick up kid. The costume jewelry Ali wore around his neck and on his fingers worked like a charm. Ali hoped the dude that killed her mother would be just as easy. Ali kept his hopes to a minimum.

# 8

## Waterbury, CT

The inferno downpour soaked anyone caught in it. At seven in the morning, the sky was dark. It looked like it promised miserable weather. The traffic on East Main Street was horrendous because there were two car accidents. Anyone in their right mind wanted to escape into the confines of their homes; the rain was getting heavier by the minute.

Mercedes drove nervously through the north end of Waterbury. Claude and Zane were crouched in the back seat to avoid being spotted. The price tags over their heads were still in full effect, and neither one of them couldn't afford a breach. Mercedes didn't know about the robbery, but she heard of Domino and Twalique's disappearance along with everyone else. She was thankful Claude and Zane were playing an incognito role. Association bred similarity and she didn't want any part of a bullet that wasn't meant for her.

After Mercedes parked in the parking lot of the morgue off of East Farm Street, Claude put on his shades and a fisherman's hat. Zane wore a baseball cap. Her hair was styled in a bob. Zane cut her dreads to avoid detection, and most importantly, to avoid an early grave. Her dreads were her trademark, and they would have betrayed her. Since the moment had arrived, Zane had second thoughts.

Zane said, "C, I'm straight. I changed my mind. I don't want to see him like that. Everything is all set. My friend Mindy is waiting in the rear entrance. She will..."

"You coming with me Zane. What the fuck? You coming in from South Carolina, and it would just defeat the entire purpose of you being here. Its not like we can go to the funeral," Claude said sternly while walking hastily to the entrance of the funeral home.

Zane mulled about going in. She wasn't a stranger to death, but seeing Tommy in the morgue was something different because it was close to home.

"I didn't know him like that so you already know I'm not going in," Mercedes said.

They ignored her and left the car without saying another word. Zane wanted to shit a brick. There was no turning back. Claude could be persistent, and she wasn't in the mood to argue with him. Mercedes watched the pair through her weed-ridden eyes, and thanked the heavens she didn't have to see a corpse.

Tommy's naked body lay prone on a slab, and it looked bloated and unrecognizable. Multiple stab wounds marked his face and body. Someone destroyed him, and from the look of his body, it was with determination, and out of malice. Zane couldn't take viewing it any longer, and she stormed out of the morgue. Claude continued to gaze at the body, and began to develop rage. *Who the fuck did this to you?* After kissing Tommy's body on the forehead, he walked away and handed Cindy, the only porter in the morgue, five hundred dollars for letting them in.

...

Zane and Mercedes slept soundly in a lodge on the Berlin Turnpike. Zane wept in Mercedes arms hours after seeing Tommy's cut body on the slab. Now, the women were asleep, leaving Claude to ponder the mysterious circumstances surrounding Tommy's murder. Claude couldn't sleep. He didn't smoke Black and Milds, but he took one from Mercedes's pack. Claude wanted to stand clear from weed and cannabis wax; he'd be damned if he was caught slipping. Claude was in hostile territory, and associates would sell him out for a hefty price.

Claude didn't think Chester had it in him to kill Tommy, but did he? Did Calvin have a hand in it? Questions swirled in his head, and he had no answers to any of them. The circumstances were strikingly similar to Rocks. It could have been from the hands of one of two enemies. The odds were against Claude and the remaining members of his team. They weren't backing down; it was fight or die.

# 9

## Los Angeles

Detectives Taft and Rinaldi had a team of law enforcement at their rear. They moved discreetly up the stairs of the dilapidated Skid Row apartment, as they all prepared to bring a murder suspect into custody, or go to war with him. Rinaldi got word that Ali Ward frequented the apartment, and police were relying on a CI's statement. Taft had a gut feeling Ali wasn't there, so he kept his hope to a minimum. Rinaldi was convinced Ali was only a few hundred yards away from them, but Taft never took Ali to be stupid.

"We are wasting valuable police time with this horse shit," Taft whispered to Rinaldi. The two detectives and the rest of the fuzz moved stealthily with their guns drawn.

"Two years is valuable time that we missed looking for Ward. Tonight, we don't give him any more time. Its time we rid the streets of all these have nots and stuff them in a can," Rinaldi said.

Taft knew that his partner wanted Ali Ward more than anything, but his veteran police instinct kicked in the second they entered the parking lot. He had a feeling that Ali was long gone.

Taft thought that he was going to retire after one of the most puzzling cases of his career two years ago. The hunt for Ali Ward enticed him out of his decision to retire. Taft's wife was beyond pissed, and she spent a great deal of time away from him. Taft felt the tension every time he stepped foot into the house, which was why he worked countless hours at the station. Taft often counseled many officers about balancing married life and work, but now Taft was going through a crisis with his own marriage. Taft never spoke on it, but Rinaldi sensed it.

Detective Rinaldi divorced his wife. Rinaldi knew she was whoring around, but seeing it up close and personal was different. It fucked him up. Rinaldi watched helplessly from outside of his bedroom window as his brother rammed his cock into her while she hummed on the second guy's dick. Rinaldi didn't know who his brother's friend was, but he was in his home, and on his mattress. Rinaldi's wife thought he was out of town. Out of rage, Rinaldi smashed the low-rise bedroom window, drew his pistol, and demanded for them to leave. The threesome walked into the night naked as the day they were born.

It had been six months since Rinaldi signed the divorce papers. He fought the hurt, loneliness, and bitterness by thinking of Ali's whereabouts. Ali's elusiveness angered him.

Six minutes later, Taft, Rinaldi, and law enforcement walked back to their cruisers empty handed. A young Hispanic woman holding an infant had opened the door after one of the cops knocked on it. They searched the entire apartment, and only found a sleeping toddler in the playpen. Taft wasn't fazed by the result because he knew Ali wasn't in the apartment.

The detectives drove back to the station in silence. Rinaldi hated the fact that Taft was right; it was nothing new.

## 10

## Waterbury

Chester zoned out while he took pulls of the piff as Murisa, the chubby Bosnian, ran her mouth. Her chunky nude body no longer turned him on because he busted all over her stomach. She gossiped to relieve her own stress in life. He paid her no attention as Murisa rambled about shit he cared less about.

Chester's residence at Angel Drive lacked furniture, but it was doable, and it posed as the perfect front. His cash was long enough to cop a six-figure crib, but Chester wasn't a dummy. Link taught him well. Chester never flossed. He was a hard working, blue collared man to the naked eye, but those that knew better, Chester was just as cold hearted as his uncle.

Link was the closest male relative he had. The more he thought of Link, the more determined Chester was to get at Claude and everyone involved in his uncle's murder. His vendetta with Claude and his team was deep. Vengeance for his uncle's killers was his number one priority, but now, Calvin's money grew longer the more he stared at it. He was paid two hundred thousand to pick up Salazar, bring him to one of Tommy's most frequented places, and drive him away after the kill. Since Link was long gone, and was unable to bring the cronies to Calvin, Chester made sure he resumed responsibility. Unlocking Link's phone after his funeral was the best thing he did, because he now had open access to all of Link's connects, including Calvin. If he followed his instructions, he would be a millionaire. Chester wanted to squeeze as much out of Calvin as he could before becoming useless to him.

"Why don't you roll another one of those spliffs? A few tokes of that and my pussy is wet," Murisa said seductively.

Chester seemed annoyed by her question, and she sensed it. Chester was short, dark, stocky, and unattractive. Murisa was broke and didn't know the next time she'd smoke.

"On second thought, I'm straight. Another one of those and I'll be out. You'll be bringing me home in the morning," Murisa said.

Chester knew she was full of shit, but he wasn't going to check her on it. He never had a threesome before, and Murisa was going to make it happen. Besides, she had some decent pussy.

Chester smiled, took a pull of the exotic, and patted her on her doughy ass.

"Too bad your home girl couldn't slide through with you. This big fat cock has enough room for the both of you." She giggled as he spoke.

"I know daddy, but she had to pick up some friends from the airport yesterday," Murisa said.

"What does that got to do with you? You ain't her number one priority? And that was yesterday. What happened to today?" Chester seemed irate.

"Why it got to be like that Michael? I think the situation her friend is in takes more precedence than your fantasy threesome," Murisa said bluntly.

"What could be more pressing than my fantasy?" Chester didn't like her tone.

Murisa said, "Smuggling two people from OT is super serious, unlike your stupid threesome fantasy. I've been in a few, and it is not all that, especially when a nigga can't fuck."

"Well, that was *your* experience, not mine. My cock is fit to please for two," Chester said arrogantly.

"Oh please, don't flatter yourself," she said as she turned around in the bed to face him. "I allow you to take charge because I know you like to feel on top of the world."

"With my self made luck, I will be on top of the world. And lets get back to your friend. What the fuck?

Is she working in the Mexican cartel? She trying to set up shop in CT?" He found himself hilarious as he laughed at his own joke.

Murisa said, "Worse. You ever hear of Claude and Zane?"

Chester's attention was at the highest peak of the night. Chester wasn't sure he heard her correctly. What were the chances of a jump-off having the vital information he needed? Chester had to put on a front. He was thankful she didn't know his real name, because Murisa would have probably made a connection since the ordeal was public knowledge.

Chester said, "Vaguely. I work and come home. I don't listen to none of that shit. What happened?"

"This didn't come from me, but I overheard Mercedes talking to that chick Zane on the phone before she picked her up from the airport. People on the street want them dead because they killed some dude named Link, and are responsible for Twalique and Domino's disappearance." Chester shifted his position in the bed, grabbed a mini Dutch, and gutted it. Now it would be a great time to smoke.

Chester said, "Once again, I am yearning for that threesome. You need to bless a nigga if you want anymore of this brain buster shit. This shit ain't cheap you know."

She looked at him and snarled her face, but Chester was right. She didn't contribute a dime to the green medicine, and she should be grateful.

"I think she at some hotel on the Berlin Turnpike. It's called something *"Arms"* or something like that, but let her do her baby, and lets do *us* tonight. We'll have plenty of time for all of that later," Marisa said as she stroked his dick until it became erect. She positioned Chester's meaty cock near her lips, and teased him with her tongue before putting the whole thing in her mouth. Chester was so pumped by the surprise news that he ejaculated into Murisa's mouth after she sucked him off for three minutes. The thought of all that money Calvin would give Chester kept his dick hard. Ignoring the condom on the junk drawer, he flipped Murisa over, inserted his dick, and gave Marisa the fuck of her life.

# 11

## Waterbury

Zane and Mercedes engaged in small talk. Mercedes told Zane that she could take the rental car when they reached Mercedes's house. Mercedes was at the wheel and didn't mind giving up the car; she could be out of sight, out of mind. Claude was back at the hotel asleep. Mercedes felt a sense of relief because she was finally getting out of the duo's presence. Claude and Zane were hot, and they created a tension so thick and deadly that they were wanted dead on first sight. Mercedes figured she was moving out of the way of the crosshair that was deadlocked on Claude, Zane, and Tank. She wanted no part of it.

Mercedes said, "I have to get away from this bitch. She wants me to do a threesome with a nigga she don't think is attractive. How the fuck does that sound?"

"Who? What he look like?" Zane laughed.

"Like a monster! I honestly don't see what Murisa sees in him!" Mercedes shook her head and bent over in laughter while she eased the car onto Bank Street in downtown Waterbury. Zane was edgy, but not to Mercedes untrained eye.

Downtown Waterbury seemed void, but silence

always spoke volumes. Zane wanted to get rid of Mercedes and flee back into hiding, but now was the time to test Mercedes loyalty. Mercedes was aware of Link and Ty's murder, and Domino and Twalique's disappearance, and those responsible behind them, but Zane had to know where Mercedes head was. Claude felt uncomfortable because Mercedes was aware. Mercedes was the second piece of pussy Claude had when he finished fifteen years of being incarcerated, but now, Claude felt disdain, and he repeatedly bashed Zane for including one of her jump offs in the mix. If Claude had known that Zane had no other option but to include Mercedes, he would have made the arrangement.

"Did you ever tell Murisa about us?" Zane asked.

Mercedes stopped in front of the red light. She felt offended, but understood Zane's position.

"Not a word," Mercedes said honestly.

Zane looked at her suspiciously, but she saw no traces of deception.

"But she was over there the other day when we spoke on the phone," Zane said carefully.

"She was knocked out Zane," Mercedes said confidently. "That bitch wouldn't have heard a gun fight."

The women laughed. Zane felt a good sense of relief. They joked and laughed some more about the dude Murisa wanted Mercedes to fuck. Zane's laughter faded the more Mercedes described him. The man Murisa wanted Mercedes to take to bed reminded Zane of Chester, but she pushed the feeling to the side. After Mercedes changed the subject, Zane became hip to the truck following them; Mercedes was oblivious. Zane thought she was being paranoid, and she wanted to test it.

"Hang this quick right," Zane ordered.

Mercedes made the turn, a quick left, and another right. The driver of the black Suburban followed them through every turn. Mercedes picked up on it and panicked.

"Zane, what the fuck? We are being followed!" Fear splintered Mercedes' heart.

Zane knew she had to think fast. Mercedes was going to be useless. Zane wished they had time to swap seats, but she had to rely on Mercedes to lose the bastard. She demanded Mercedes to lose the driver, called Claude, and waited for him to pick up. The phone rang multiple times before he answered it.

"C, these fuckers are following us!" Zane shouted.

Claude sat up in the bed quickly, and adjusted his phone.

"Zane, can you see the driver?" Claude asked.

Claude was losing her. The connection was close to being lost. He could only hear tidbits of her fear-stricken voice.

"I can't hear you, but if you could hear me, don't panic..." Claude yelled her name continuously.

Claude heard the car crash. He yelled her name, but no response. Thirty seconds later, Claude heard a single gunshot, ruffling noises, and tires screeching. And the phone disconnected. Claude called back six times, and kept getting her voicemail. He got out of the bed, and started to pace ferociously. Claude was literally stuck. He had no car or weapon. Claude slowed his pace to ease the fear so he could think. He was running out of time. If either of the women caught the bullet, someone more than likely had one of them at gunpoint and was on their way; however, the gunshot painted a grim picture.

After packing his bag, Claude walked out of the hotel room, paid for it, and started walking on the Berlin Turnpike. His mind was swirling with uncertainty. He didn't know who was shot, but he had a feeling Zane was alive, and being used as bait. In a disturbing way, Mercedes's death would be a relief to him. Claude felt that she was a breach from the start, and that her presence increased their chance of all of them getting killed.

Cars whizzed by Claude on the turnpike as he walked it at four in the morning. The morning was void and quiet. The gunshot he heard rang loud in his head. He gritted his teeth with the thought of Zane leaking blood. Claude knew Calvin had his hand in it, but Link, Domino, and Twalique's allies wanted their heads.

The sun was rising. After walking an hour and a half, Claude checked himself into another hotel in Meriden. Claude dropped his bag and sat down. He rubbed his hands over his head, and continued to fear for Zane's life. Claude's cell phone yanked him out of his thoughts. The caller was just the man Claude wanted to talk to. He was the one that told Claude Tommy was killed. Claude tried him earlier, but the caller wasn't available. He didn't want to include the old man, but he had no other choice.

## 12

## Meriden, CT

Claude waited anxiously for his guest to arrive. It had been forty-five minutes since he checked into the Marriott, and Claude's feet were killing him from walking three miles. During his wait, Claude turned on the television, and he channel surfed to the news. The shooting he heard over the phone was headline. Mercedes's picture was plastered on the television. The anchorman revealed that there were no witnesses, and the suspect(s) were still at large. Claude was relieved that it wasn't Zane's picture on the news. Zane was somewhere in bondage, and Claude would die trying to find her.

Claude flinched and gripped his gun when he heard the knocking. He walked to the door without throwing caution into the wind despite having an idea who it was. Claude looked through the peephole. Lester stood outside the door coughing. He was thinner, disheveled, and unhealthy. When Claude opened the door, he embraced his friend as if he didn't notice the jaundice in his face. He was just glad Lester came through.

"How's it been old man?" Claude asked.

Lester smiled and revealed missing teeth.

"Getting old, but I'm good as long as this bad liver can hold up."

Claude didn't know how to respond. The last time he had seen Lester, he was at full strength, and working hard as a porter at the hospital. Lester was there for Claude when he was abruptly relieved of his duties. Most importantly, Lester provided Claude with the connections that gave him the tools he used to kill his adversaries.

"Cirrhosis of the liver man. Count your blessings," Lester said.

"Besides money and family, I don't have too much to count. As of right now, niggas is coming for my throat," Claude said, getting straight to the point.

There was no time for formalities. Lester already knew about Domino and Twalique's disappearance, and Link and Ty's demise, but he didn't know about the money Claude stole from Calvin. Claude filled in the blanks. If anyone knew the streets, Calvin was a legend, but to Lester, Calvin was just a pawn in the underworld. It didn't surprise him that Claude and his team stuck him for his money and jewels. Lester listened as Claude ran the rest down to him.

"Just like they came after Tommy's throat. I figured you were involved when I got your message.

This is some heavy shit young blood," Lester said seriously, stroking on his gray goatee.

Claude rubbed his hand across his face out of distress. He looked directly into Lester's eyes. Lester may not be fit for combat, but his resources were thick and valuable.

Claude said, "I need your help Les. I'm putting something together, and I can't do it without you. I need to find Zane 'cause the niggas that snatched her killed that Puerto Rican chick you saw on the news."

He gave Lester a chance to absorb the information he dropped on him. Lester's expression didn't change nor was he surprised. Lester was an old G, and been around life altering drama his entire life. Before Lester got a chance to utter a response, Claude's phone vibrated on the table. He cursed because it was about to die, and his charger was in Zane's possession. It was a call from Zane's cell. The men looked at each other quizzically. Lester beckoned Claude to answer it, and to put in on speaker.

Claude said, "Yo."

"C, what up? I'm finally hearing your voice, but too bad it is under these dire circumstances. And yeah, we got your dyke bitch. In a few seconds, you'll receive a text. And you let ME know who is playing games. Since you are in the business of making niggas disappear and killing my people, I'm going to make this carpet munchin' bitch vanish if you don't bring yourself and everything you stole from Calvin. You got a week." The phone disconnected.

Claude could do nothing but stare at it. When the text surfaced, it came with an attachment. After opening it, anger overcame him. The message that came with the attachment placed Claude's anger and fear on a higher plateau. It read *Now who is playing games?* It was a picture of Zane roped, gagged, bruised, bleeding, and unconscious. Claude dropped the phone, grabbed the desk, and made an attempt to toss it across the room. Lester intervened just in time.

"To answer your question, yes, I will help you. But for now, you have to calm down and think this thing through. Who was that?"

Claude came down off his spurt of anger, and he began to put things in perspective. He knew exactly who it was.

"Chester, Link's nephew."

Lester said, "She's alive C. If they wanted to kill her, she'd be dead by now. We need to think."

Lester sat Claude down and drilled him. The situation was sticky, but Lester never lost his touch.

Claude gave him more detail. He brought Lester up to speed on what was going on. Claude thanked the Gods that Lester was still alive and was willing to help him.

"Les, how could I repay you bro? I got you on that paper. I'm forever indebted to you fam," Claude said sincerely.

Lester stopped in his tracks and smiled. He saw himself in Claude. Lester was in his shoes, and knew how grateful the young man was. Claude was a fighter, and it would take a lot of war to make him wobble.

"C, what the fuck do I got to lose? Either somebody gives me their liver, or I live six more months. And if I only got six months to live, then I want to go out in a blaze of glory," Lester said.

"You silly ass motherfucker. After this shit is done, you'll have enough cash to buy you a new liver. Fuck that blaze of glory shit. When we lay these niggas to rest, we going to be funky rich. And you ain't dyin' bro," Claude said convincingly.

Lester felt that, but kept his usual hostile face. Other than his son, he had no one in his corner for his numbered days on the planet. Dying alone scared him more than death itself. The only thing that Lester had left in the world was his balls, and a death sentence.

He was going to ride with Claude.

The men walked out of the hotel. Claude checked out of it while Lester waited in the car. During their travel, they exchanged ideas about their plan of rescuing Zane and sending Calvin, Chester, and whoever was involved to their graves.

## 13

## Greenwich, CT

Percy Wetmore couldn't believe he was socializing with the elites of Wall Street, pro athletes, fashion designers, and directors. A thin and bearded Caucasian man was across the living room playing the violin, creating a comfortable mood amongst the swank guests in the mansion. Percy was smart, and he had the gift of gab, but he was nothing more then a two-bit hustler. He wasn't shit, but his exterior prevented anyone from exposing him.

Percy accumulated some fame as of late. Two years ago, while driving from Stamford, Connecticut, he was being pursued relentlessly by Domincans. The chase ended when he ran over and killed a woman. In a high profile lengthy vehicular murder trial, the jury rewarded Percy a not guilty verdict, sparing him a minimum fifteen year sentence. Due to mishaps with evidence, tampered surveillance tapes, and inconsistent testimony, Percy beat his vehicular murder case. Mitigating factors won over the jury, and they rewarded him freedom.

Percy went from sitting in New Haven County to rubbing shoulders with the upper class, even though it was by default. Sherry Hemmingway, a short obese

Italian woman, was sitting on top of her cash alone. She was a CEO on Wall Street, and was worth millions. Despite her long money, she was unattractive, insecure, and lonely. No one at or above her status would give her the time of day, but there was an open market of felons that would utilize her wealthy lifestyle.

Sherry fell in love with Percy the second she laid eyes on him. Percy caught her eye while he played the numbers at a gas station in South Norwalk. Although he avoided a life long ban from society a week prior, Percy was an ex-con with a past, and could read vulnerabilities in anybody. Sherry's vulnerability was her appearance. She was five foot two, and weighed over three hundred pounds. Loose folds of skin could be seen through her t-shirt, but Percy looked beyond that. He looked at the car she poured gas in. It was a 2017 Jaguar.

While engaged in conversation at the gas pump, Percy saw the Visa Black card Sherry pulled out of her Louis Vuitton handbag to pay for her gas. The next day, Percy was pulling down her panties over her doughy legs. He moved in her million-dollar home a month later, and has been there ever since. He was living large a year after his acquittal.

Percy admired the Georgian Colonial style house that was situated in a low-key community. The bricks date back to 1836. Percy saw the small writing engraved in the patio while Sherry spoke to a yuppie couple about trades and stocks on the lawn earlier. An influx of mosquitos forced everyone indoors at the private party as the day waned.

High profile people stood around and talked politics, sports, and stats. Percy and Sherry stood side by side with Harold, an aging politician who spoke of Earl Nightingale's *The Strangest Secret*. The frail man spoke about success, and how failure was not an option in his world.

"Once your mind is deeply rooted and steeped in negativity, it will always be a misfortune for anyone thinking that kind of way," the man said.

"Absolutely," Percy rebounded before anyone else took a crack at the topic. "People are not successful because of the way they think. They tend to conform to other people, and they lack the heart, drive, and motivation to step away from what everyone else is doing. It takes courage to do your own thing, but everyone is afraid of moving away from the masses." Percy said that with a serious face. Sherry was proud how Percy conducted himself around the big faces. In private, Percy was rough around the edges, and she found that sexy. Her pussy got wet listening to her man blend in a conversation that everyone probably thought he knew nothing about.

Sherry's best friend Heather looked on, and she saw the happiness in Sherry's face. Heather found Percy handsome. He was tall, dark, dreaded, muscular, and had a well-groomed goatee. The more she watched Percy in action, the more convinced she became of his motive. Heather knew he beat a murder rap, and that he had a prison history. Heather knew her friend was blinded by Percy's charm, but she wasn't. Heather could see right through him. He didn't have two dollars in his wallet when they met. Now Percy lived in a mansion. Heather thought that to be too convenient. Since Sherry was the rightful owner of the residence, she decided it would be best to keep her opinion about Sherry's boyfriend to herself. Sherry would see what was beneath the mask in due time.

...

Ali smiled when Percy stepped out of the mansion like he owned it. He watched Percy light up a cigarette, and exhale like he was king shit. In reality, he was living on borrowed time. Percy unintentionally killed Raven's mother, and got away with it. Ali was ready to cut his glory short and serve as his Grim Reaper. Ali won't get Percy tonight, but he planned on cutting Percy's lights out soon. After Percy went back into the lavish home, Ali put the notepad to the side and drove away. Ali was satisfied of today's progress.

## 14

## Miami, Florida/Cheshire, Connecticut

Calvin relaxed on the deck of the thirtieth floor of the boutique hotel overlooking the Atlantic Ocean. He escaped the tranquility, and the serene nature of the sea to chill out at the high-end hotel. Calvin sighed arrogantly as he enjoyed the fruits of his labor. Calvin sipped his Jack Daniels and thought of all the people he crossed, friends he betrayed, adversaries he tortured, and the enemies he murdered. Calvin paid his dues, and he was seriously contemplating retirement. He wanted to spend the rest of his days raising his child, and fucking his beautiful wife. His small smirk thinking of the future turned into a hideous snarl on his hostile, ugly face. Calvin stroked at the mole on his left temple, and wondered how Chester and Salazar were handling the situation.

Since Calvin stepped into the underworld, he was feared and respected. Claude was an exception; he wasn't afraid of Calvin, and that's what pecked at his think tank whenever it was idle. Calvin found Claude, took it to him with a hired assassin, and Claude countered by killing Bam. Claude even sent pictures as proof. Calvin painfully respected that. If Claude could murder two and make another two disappear the same night, then God only knew what he was capable of. Calvin felt the dire need to protect Jessica and their child. Claude felt the same way about his family. It was like a knife fight when no one backed down. He had to remove Claude from the planet, and to do so quickly.

Calvin's advisor Lionel told him he needed to swallow his pride and take it as a loss. What Claude and his people stole from him was peanuts. Lionel told Calvin to look at his vendetta like boxing. Calvin may have the resources and tools to eliminate Claude, but great boxers often fall victim to boxers with grit, heart, and determination. Calvin didn't need a gritty nemesis in his life, but he was too hell bent on revenge to see the overall picture.

Jessica lay in the chair next to him reading a cosmetic magazine while wearing shades. Calvin secretly looked at the side of her face and got an erection. She was beyond beautiful, but it only added more fuel to his insecurities. Calvin knew he wasn't an attractive man, and Jessica wouldn't have wasted a glance in his direction if Calvin didn't have money. Calvin knew that most men, if not all, looked better than him, so he kept Jessica close. Jessica wasn't allowed to go anywhere. Calvin hated visiting her parents because of their discreet glances of disgust. Calvin once killed a man for complimenting his wife. Whenever Calvin thought Jessica was looking at a man, he'd smack her, apologize, and shower Jessica with expensive gifts. Calvin knew he didn't deserve her, however, he thanked the heavens for having her as his wife.

Juan Rios, one of Calvin's many workers, destroyed Calvin's next thought with his quiet entry onto the deck. Juan hated interrupting his boss, but Salazar was on the phone. Calvin sat up and snatched the throwaway cell phone from him. When he turned his back on his worker and started talking, Juan and Jessica's eyes met. Jessica smiled and bit her lip. If she wasn't wearing shades, she would have been caught red handed looking at the suave, tall, sleek haired Hispanic. The five o'clock stubble was the icing on the cake. Juan feared Calvin, and didn't want any trouble. Juan averted his eyes, and walked back into the safety of the hotel without looking back.

When he was done with his conversation with Salazar, Calvin rose out of his comfort zone. He showered, shaved, shitted, packed, and instructed Juan to take him and two other goons to his private jet. The plot was getting thick in Connecticut, and that was the destination. Calvin vowed that he wouldn't leave the state until Claude stopped breathing.

...

Tank and his bunkmate Jewelz were playing chess. Tank stared intensely at the board as he calculated a future move on it. Chess was the only thing keeping his mind off of Tommy and Mercedes, and the fact that his calls were going straight to Claude's voicemail.

Tommy and Mercedes death hit the prison as soon as it happened. A few days ago, Tommy's murder was the hot topic. Now Mercedes shared the spotlight. She was the sister of Pedro, a correctional officer who worked the graveyard shift. Tank knew he wouldn't see Pedro unless he planned on doing another bid. Tank was due to be discharged within a week, and he hoped he could obtain information about her murder. Tank knew Mercedes. He met her the night Darlene got jumped. Mercedes was one of the attackers. Mercedes was with her friend Diamond. Tank remembered Claude linking up with Mercedes, and Rocks connecting with Diamond that night. He remembered going home alone.

Tank wondered if Claude and Zane were with her when Mercedes got popped. Tank tried not to imagine the worst for his comrades, but in his mind, Tommy's murder was a blatant warning for revenge. The thought pulled at Tank's conscious all day, and he was thankful Jewelz helped him relieve his uncertainty by kicking his ass in chess.

Tank moved the rook in the direct path of the king. He flashed a grin.

"Checkmate," Tank said.

"Fuck," Jewelz said. He used the collar of his jumper to wipe the sweat off his brow. "Run it back."

Jewelz was a short, dark burly man with a thick beard. He handed the honey bun to Tank before setting the pieces back on the board. It was their fourth game. Jewelz was a gunrunner from Bridgeport, and Tank wanted his services. Despite being incarcerated, Jewelz had someone on the outside intercepting the gun and ammunition supply. He was due to discharge by the end of the week.

"You getting better, though. Instead of me being four moves ahead of you, I'm only three," Tank said.

They shared a chuckle.

"But on another note, your man get them joints in?" Tank tried not to sound desperate.

Jewelz said, "Still no answer on that bro. He been waitin' for days, but if I'm out before you, I got you. I got your math."

"Alright, no rush fam," Tank lied. He needed those guns badly. "Just checkin' the status, but in the meantime, take this ass whippin' like a man."

Later on that evening, Tank tried to reach Claude, but his phone went straight to voice mail. Tank tried calling him repeatedly despite the hostile faces behind him waiting to use the jack. Tank hung up the phone and walked away to avoid trouble. He had more pressing shit to worry about.

# 15

## Waterbury

Quotes of inspiration and anything recovery related adorned the walls of the halfway house. Residents cleaned the kitchen, swept and mopped the hallways, smoked outside, and watched TV. The program director and the case managers were having a meeting inside the program director's office, leaving one case manager to hold down the fort.

Delores Porter answered every question the case manager read to her from the old model COMPAQ computer screen. Under normal circumstances, a person would view the halfway house as a step away from total freedom. Delores thought otherwise. Tank wasn't the only one flooded with uncertainty. Delores hadn't slept properly since she spoke to Sahara a day after Claude's abrupt departure from the Bahamas. It had been two weeks. Sahara spared Delores about the assassin Claude pushed off the planet. Sahara told her mother Claude was in town to say goodbye to Tommy, and to settle some unfinished business. Sahara's comment about Claude settling unfinished business sent chills down her spine. Delores had a feeling that Tommy's death was going to lure Claude out of hiding. Claude being in town meant bloodshed, and Delores felt useless because she would be living at the halfway house for the next six months.

After Kevin finished her intake, he told her what the expectations were. Delores saw the way Kevin looked at her, and she wasn't impressed. She'd been down for seventeen years, and the aging gods took care of her beauty. She put on a little weight over the years, but she looked good. Her breasts were plump. She had a few streaks of gray in her long cornrows that touched the small of her back. Her light skin was youthful and flawless. Kevin saw that and wouldn't mind a taste.

"You have any questions for me?" Kevin asked.

Delores saw the seduction in his eyes.

"How long do I have to be in here before I could start looking for jobs?" Delores was looking for any opportunity to ride or die with her son, and to provide as much help with the limited time she had outside the halfway house.

"Thirty days. And then you meet with the team and present yourself in front of us on why you think you deserve a chance to start looking for employment. If you can get past that, you can start looking for jobs," Kevin said.

Delores provided no reaction. Despite what was

going on, spending thirty days inside the halfway house was a lot better than the seventeen calendars she spent in Niantic. When Kevin was ready to throw her a little game, the phone in the office rang.

"Connecticut Recovery...yeah...yes she is, but next time call on the payphone...its ok...hold on," Kevin said before handing her the phone.

She received the phone reluctantly before speaking into it.

"Hello?"

"Ma, don't speak, just listen carefully. We'll do all the formalities later."

Claude allowed the silence to linger before proceeding.

"Yes or no. Was that Kevin that answered the phone?" Claude asked.

"Yes."

"You heard about that Spanish chick that got murdered on I-691?" Claude was pretty sure she heard about the murder.

"Yes." Delores followed suit quickly. She did the same thing whenever there were ear hustlers around. Kevin shifted through paperwork, but his ears were wide open. Delores instilled that phone code shit in her children years ago. Listening to her son reminded her on how much they were alike. Delores felt that something was wrong and out of place.

Claude asked, "Does anyone in there know I'm your son?"

"I don't know." Delores was growing gravely concerned. She felt pain in the pit of her stomach.

"Find out quietly," Claude said. Delores knew that meant finding out without opening her mouth.

Delores said, "Okay."

"When are visiting hours?" Claude asked.

"Kevin, when are visiting hours?" Delores asked, ignoring the stupid, lustful look Kevin had on his face.

"The weekends is *one to four* and *six to eight* throughout the week," Kevin said loud enough for Claude to hear him.

"Got it," Claude said. "Somebody will be down there tomorrow at six to drop you off a phone, info, and cash."

"Okay," Delores said, looking at Kevin to see if he wasn't minding his business. Kevin kept his eyes on one of the inmate's charts.

"Find dirt on homeboy Ma," Claude said.

"I will." Tears spilled down her face. Delores didn't know the details of her son's ordeal, but she felt death lurking around the corner.

"Keep your eyes and ears open. I gotta go. I love you Ma," Claude said.

"I love you too baby," Delores reciprocated before Claude hung up.

Delores gave Kevin back the phone, and she wiped the tears off of her youthful face. She was a woman hardened by nature, but she loved her family more than anything. Underneath her tough exterior, she was scared to death. Delores murdered once, and she would do it again to protect her son.

Kevin didn't know what was said on the phone, but he eliminated his flirtatious tone...for now.

"Everything okay?" Kevin asked with fake sincerity.

Delores had to get dirt on him and fast. The more she looked at him, the more she wanted to vomit. Kevin was thirty-nine, but he looked a lot older. He was light skinned, and his eyes looked like they were going to fall from his sockets. When Delores saw the dirt and grime in his nails, she cringed. Any woman willing to give that man some pussy would be a desperate bitch. Two of his teeth were chipped, and a few were caked with plaque.

"I'm okay. Just everyday shit, you know what I mean?" Delores wanted to get Kevin out of her face.

"I know exactly what you mean, but I'm glad you're okay," he said. Kevin wasn't due to start his new third shift position until early next week, but he planned to hump some pussy. He was fucking one of the clients on the residential side, but Kevin had his eyes on Delores.

Delores and Kevin left the office. He escorted her to her bed, ran some more rules and regulations by her, flirted, and left her alone amongst the other residents. Delores scanned the few faces in the dorm, and didn't recognize anyone, which was a good thing, but there were many residents in the work release and residential side that she didn't come across yet. Putting her fear, anxiety, and uncertainty to the side, Delores lay on the bed, and started to scheme her move on Kevin.

...

Delores waited for her guest in the drizzle. The rain felt great to her. It eased a little of the tension she had within herself. The conversation she had with her son spooked her. Delores bummed a cigarette from a resident, and she quickly craved another one after she put the butt out. She'd do anything to ease the animosity and fear she carried at the pit of her stomach.

The residents were enjoying their visits. Relatives and friends hugged, couples held hands, and children enjoyed their loved ones. Delores waited anxiously for the unknown visitor. She looked out for a 2005 Green Honda Accord. Her focus was set on the entrance of the halfway house. When Delores saw the car round the corner, her anxiety peeked. The driver found a spot to park, stepped out the car, and walked towards Delores. He looked familiar. The closer he got, the more familiar he looked. And then it hit her. He approached her with a *Stop & Shop* bag in his hand, and a smile on his face.

"It's been a long time Lester. How are you?" Judging by his sickly appearance, he didn't seem to be doing well. She recounted his glory days as a stick up kid, drug dealer, and murderer.

They embraced.

"Ill get to that at another time Delores, but right now, we need to talk," he said as he handed her the bag. She looked inside of it. There were four boxes of Newport, an IPhone, and a thick wad of cash. Instead of going inside the building, Delores and Lester walked off to the side of the house. Her ears were opened, and she remained tight-lipped. Lester drilled her from start to finish about Claude's road of destruction to Zane's kidnapping.

After the visit, Delores was numb, stressed, and scared, but remained poised around the residents. She refused to pass any judgment about her son. Delores didn't care how many people Claude stuck in the dirt. She was riding with him, and would help him put more people in their plots to remain alive if that was what it took. When Kevin crossed her line of sight, she knew she had to put her plan in motion, or watch her son war from the sideline.

## 16

## Hartford, CT/ Coral Harbour

The basement was musky, cold, and damp. No one lived in the building above it. The ramshackle dwelling was an eyesore, and no one frequented it. The putrid smell of the place didn't bother Zane because she contributed to it. She had feces all over the lower half of her body to keep from being raped. Zane didn't want neither of the men getting aroused. Her right eye was swollen shut. Cuts, scrapes, abrasions, and cigarette burns marked her body. She sat on the folding chair with her hands tied around the back of it.

Zane took an onslaught of punishment from one of her captors. The killing and kidnapping was business to Salazar, but it was both business and personal for Chester. He didn't have to ask about his uncle Link's death; he wanted to know what happened to Twalique and Domino. Chester tried to beat it out of her. Salazar had to admit that Zane was a tough bitch. She hadn't said a word since their arrival despite being tortured. Chester placed the gag back over Zane's mouth and tested her restraint. Satisfied with its security, the two men left the basement without saying a word.

Zane was alone with her fearful thoughts. She

was certain the men were going to kill her, but she knew they needed her alive. Mercedes death didn't weigh on Zane yet, for she was fearful of her own life. Her exterior was tough, and it gained Salazar's respect, but Zane was afraid of the murderous charged men.

Hours later, Zane tensed up when the men returned. She felt the chill from Chester's cold glare. If Calvin didn't have a plan, he would have easily killed her, but that wasn't part of it. Without any sign or warning, Chester smacked her viciously across her face, and drew more blood. He wasn't allowed to kill her yet, but Calvin said nothing about hurting the bitch. Chester smacked her some more before grabbing her jaw, and pulling her face close to his. Zane could smell the stench of weed and alcohol on his breath. Chester looked in Zane's eyes with a crazed, calm look.

"Where did y'all dump them bodies?" Chester's body locked up with rage.

When Zane didn't answer, Chester wound his arm back to strike again, but Salazar grabbed Chester's arm before Chester could fire off a blow.

"Amigo, lets stick to the plan. Leave her alone... for now," Salazar said smoothly. He understood

Chester's position, but he'd be damned if Chester fucked it up for him. There was too much money on the table to be on some personal shit. After Salazar redirected Chester away from her and out of the basement, Zane secretly embraced death. Her hope and faith was riding on fumes.

...

Mark felt stunned; it was hard for him to keep his composure around the women, especially Sahara. He walked on the beach with a rolled up stick of piff in his right hand. Zane's kidnapping destroyed any hope of Claude leaving Connecticut alive. Claude updated Mark on the shit that was popping off, but the women, besides Sahara, didn't know of Zane's disappearance. Sonya and Fatima didn't know Zane, but knew she was close to home. If Mark had revealed that to Sonya, she would have fallen over the deep end.

Mark decided to go for a walk because of the tension mounting in the beach house. Fatima threatened to take their child, and head back to Texas. Mark lost it, forcing her to see another side of him that she had never seen. Mark felt horrible for speaking to her coldly, but she needed to hear it.

The sounds of the ocean normally had a calming effect on Mark. It provided him the tranquility he needed. Today was different. He couldn't shake Zane's kidnapping. The moonlight exposed a few couples and individual stragglers who walked the beach at night. Mark found a spot on the soft sand, pulled out his gun, made sure the safety was on, tucked it under his thigh, and sat down. He felt bloodshed in his bones, and he could do nothing but wait.

# 17

## Brooklyn

Ali's demons invaded him while he slept. Images of Simone's corpse and his son crying next to her tormented him. Ali saw their images at night when he slept, and he felt the burden of guilt during the day when he walked. He tossed, turned, and cursed on the couch while Raven watched him. They cleared the air and started getting along. In a strange way, they felt alone in the world, and they needed each other. Raven found herself falling for Ali even though she never looked at him like that. It was different in the present. Raven was playing a dirty, dangerous game, and the thought of being alone made her nauseas. Ali may be a career criminal, but he possessed qualities that turned her on. He was patient, persistent, and calculating. She never saw those set of skills in Ali until she joined him on a stakeout. Raven was restless, and she begged Ali to call it off for the night, but Ali ignored her, and watched Percy and his routine. Raven saw him as a trigger-happy hot head. It was different now. The murky aura Ali had around him turned Raven on.

She wore a purple, cozy short robe. The belt of it was loose, thus exposing one of her breasts. Raven's short hair was slicked back, and still wet from the shower. Raven's perfume was the icing on the cake. She sat at the end of the couch, and watched him while he relived his nightmare. On cue, Ali jolted out of his sleep. He leaked perspiration, and he panted excessively, looking at whom he thought was Simone. Still breathing heavily, Ali kept his eyes on the beautiful specimen. Raven saw his erection rise in his boxer shorts. That was what she wanted so badly. It sent her body into overdrive. Raven let her knees fall open, watching Ali's reaction. He stared greedily at her groomed treasure.

Ali was in a daze, unsure of what was in front of him, and whether the godly beauty was real or fiction. Ali saw the hunger in Raven's eyes. He stalked closer, her beautiful body nearing his. When Ali invaded her space, their noses touched. He kissed Raven greedily while holding her angelic face. Raven looked so sexy to him that Ali thought she was an illusion, a figment of his imagination.

When Raven crawled on top of him, and felt her tongue on his skin, Ali came to his senses and knew it was real. There was a wholly satisfying link between them. The chemistry existed, and it was deep. They tasted and sucked each other for over an hour. Raven was fascinated by Ali's thick penis. She gave him good hand and mouth work, and vice versa. Raven sucked on his nipples softly. Ali would have busted prematurely if he had been a virgin. Raven circled her hips and teased her center with his dick. She was soaked and ready for action.

Ali carried Raven out of the living room, and into the bedroom. He laid her gently on the bed. Raven's legs spread into the shape of a "V." Without hesitation, Ali tasted Raven one last time before mounting her. Raven wrapped her legs around his back. Ali stroked her softly while he kissed Raven passionately. Five minutes into the session, Ali hit a spot. Raven's nails dug deep into Ali's skin as her body jerked wildly, squirting love juices all over the comforter. Ali was so turned on by Raven's orgasm that he could have released with her, but Ali wasn't done. He didn't even crack the surface. Ali pulled out and explored Raven some more. He glared at the lust in Raven's hazel eyes before flipping her over.

Raven moaned as Ali's penis dived into her center. Ali split her ass cheeks apart, and inserted his finger in Raven's anus. The animal noises were getting louder as Ali stroked harder. He was ready to bust. Ali flipped Raven over again, inserted his dick, and pumped her voraciously. If someone heard their action, they would think that a priest was performing an exorcism. Raven was in a trance. She had access to Ali's nipples while lying on her back. She licked them slow and seductively. It drove Ali into a zone. Ali felt it coming. Raven sensed it. She consumed him as if he were the best thing she'd ever tasted. Ali gripped Raven tight, and released his orgasm into her. Raven circled her hips to receive every last drop. Ali lay on top of her. They panted from their lovemaking.

After they washed up, Ali rolled a blunt, and cuddled with her. They were silent and comfortable. Neither of them had regret. It was the start of a beginning.

"What was that about?" Raven asked as if she didn't know.

Ali took a hit, exhaled, and smiled.

"You tell me. You initiated it. I feel like you took advantage of me. I had no choice," Ali said jokingly.

"Yeah right," Raven said. She accepted the blunt from him and took a pull. "But in all seriousness, it was building up. I never looked at you like that until you got here. You drove all the way from Cali to help me. That alone was a turn on despite our circumstances, but I was curious."

Ali took a moment to absorb what Raven said.

"So there is no more curiosity. Now what?" Ali asked as he inhaled and exhaled the marijuana.

"You tell me," Raven reciprocated.

Ali smiled.

"I never knew you looked at me like that, but I always found you to be a dime. Not only that. Despite what I said to you in the past, you did come through when I needed you the most. I was fucked up and getting shitted on by Simone because of what I was only able to bring to the table." Ali meant that, but he knew his status as an outlaw, and he didn't want to set himself up. Before she got a chance to counter his statement, Ali beat her to the punch.

Ali said, "Raven, I appreciate the attraction and the sex, but I'm living on borrowed time. I'm on the run. I'll fucking get killed before I let the pigs get me. And that may more then likely happen. I'm not going to prison."

Raven understood his stance, but she didn't care. She lost her brother and mother. She had no one left besides distant relatives that she wasn't close to.

"I'm down, baby." Raven crawled on top of him. Her body felt soft to him. She felt Ali's erection. The dark room prevented her from seeing the thirst and lust in his eyes. "I'm all in til' death do us part," Raven said seriously.

Ali dug that, but he had a feeling he would care and love her too deeply to allow her to go to hell with him. He was now at a crossroads. Simone's corpse made his sleep uncomfortable. If his arrangement with Raven was real, he vowed that he would protect her. That was a lot easier said than done. Ali started to say something, but Raven cut him short by placing her finger over his lips.

"Shhh." Raven silenced him with her sensual touches, making Ali forget about where he stood.

# 18

## Kent, CT

Claude and Lester sat quietly in the hotel room checking, preparing, and loading guns. Even though the men didn't exchange dialogue, they knew what they were getting themselves into. They both knew death was a possibility. A terminal illness had a vice grip on Lester's life. Getting hit by a bullet was a better option in his mind. The only reason why Lester never stuck the barrel of the gun in his mouth was because he believed in God, Heaven, and Hell. Suicide was the most horrific sin of them all. Helping Claude on his mission to face his monsters wasn't a problem.

Claude sat on the other bed screwing on silencers. After taking a break from working on his half of the weaponry, Claude picked up his small notepad and read over his notes.

"So Les, these two dudes are kids?" Claude asked, his eyes still trained on his handwriting.

"Looks like it. Just young and stupid foot soldiers looking for a come up. Shouldn't be hard to snatch and shake 'em down. I don't know if these dudes have any kind of affiliation with Chester, but they are feared. They're sneaky, which makes them dangerous," Lester said. Claude pondered it, and believed he knew exactly who the young goons were.

"Did you tail Chester?" Claude asked.

"For three hours. Looks like he has a spot up Bucks Hill, but his actual residence is out in Cheshire. Same shit Link was on. He puts on a front as a struggling working class citizen, but behind it all, the motherfucker got cake. He ain't a dummy, I tell you that much," Lester said.

Claude never took Chester to be a dummy, but Claude knew he was smarter than him, and he knew he would probably have to kill Chester before knocking over some other pawns. Claude scribbled a few more things in the notebook, memorized what he wrote, and struck a match. Claude burned the documents before grabbing his weapons. Lester did the same.

"By the time we get to Waterbury, it will be dark. We got to get these niggas tonight," Claude said.

"So what about Tank? You hear from him?" Lester asked.

"I did. We going to get him in a bit, but for right now, let's get these rugrats," Claude said coldly.

Lester said, "We need info first Claude."

"I know, and we will get it. But after that, we kill 'em," Claude said coldly.

...

Clarence "Jack" Branch and Arnold "Fat Boy" Frost sat high and smug in an old Land Rover shooting the shit, and scheming on broads. Scantily clad chicks walked out of the hole in the wall tavern looking like they wanted to fuck anything with a cock. Thugs drove slowly down North Main stealing a glance at the action. The latest rap vibrated in the hottest Coupes and SUVs. The young thugs were in the mood for some fun, but something seemed to trouble Jack.

Jack was a flunky, born and raised in Harlem, New York, but spent most of his childhood in Waterbury. His school years consisted of truancy and violence. At twenty, he'd already done three bids, and was working on his fourth one. Jack was short and dark skinned with an influx of razor bumps on his neck. He had a massive scar on the back of his head from falling from the monkey bars as a child. Jack never amounted to anything, and his conscious was shot.

"Fat Boy" was actually medium height and rail thin. Arnold got the nickname "Fat Boy" when he was in elementary school. Fat Boy smoked cigarettes, weed, dust, and drank liquor all throughout middle school. He completed one year of high school before being a product of the streets for good. Fat Boy slimmed down because of his early age toxin intake. He wore a thick black hoody that swallowed his upper body. His hooded red eyes made him look like a menace.

Fat Boy and Jack had little history. They met under a deadly circumstance. They were hired by a major drug dealer to make a hit on another drug dealer. Since the hit was successful, it only made sense to connect on a second one. Jack reached out to Fat Boy, and it was a done deal.

Jack's cell phone ringer killed the silence in the truck. Jack looked at it, and he twisted his face. Every time his cousin called, he always wanted something.

"What nigga?" Jack asked flatly.

"Fuck you mean what? I don't need anything, but I'm looking at that dude with the price tag on his head," Gervin said.

"Word to who?" Jack asked. Jack looked at his own phone to see if what he was hearing was real.

"To everything I owe my dude," Gervin said.

Jack listened attentively as Gervin revealed his discovery.

"Yeah...ok...yeah motherfucker...yeah you going to get a cut...alright...follow that nigga," Jack said impatiently before hanging up.

Fat Boy passed Jack the blunt. Jack looked at his crime partner, and flashed his million-dollar smile.

"I told you I wasn't trippin. That dude is home from the belly bro, but we about to set him up for his home going," Jack said. He pulled out two loaded .38s from underneath the seat, and he slid the second one to Fat Boy.

"Word, but how much of a cut we given ya' cuzzo?" Fat Boy asked. Fat Boy didn't like the sound of that shit.

"Nothing that would kill our cut fam. I know where you at, and where you stand with him, but he found him," Jack said.

Fat Boy nodded his head, but he still didn't like the idea of Gervin having a hand on his grip.

They drove through Waterbury silent and tight lipped. Bad news would sweep through the Brass City soon.

# 19

## Los Angeles

Flip sat stoned faced in his 2007 Cadillac Deville stalking the dude that dropped a line on him to the police. Flip chained smoked cigarettes, and he reflected on what led him on the brink of adding another body to his resume. Flip's mind was murky and dark. He would embrace death before prison. Flip was dangerous and desperate.

Prior to his pending downfall, Flip's life was the shit since he stepped foot back in Los Angeles. Flip had done a nine-year bid in Connecticut after a botched drug deal. A month after being released, Flip pushed two people from the planet. Despite parole lingering over him, Flip left the east coast to start a life that he envisioned while incarcerated. He started slow, got big, and lived a glamour life. Flip and Ali ran the drug and gun operation like clockwork. Drugs and guns moved through dealers and killer's hands with fluidity. Yet, like any great organization, there was always a rat.

Black Ferris was young, cocky, and a loudmouth hustler who always preached death before dishonor. Black Ferris was respected and feared, and the flunkies he had in his circle praised him like a god.

When he got bagged and questioned about whom he worked for, Black Ferris threw Flip under the bus about his entire operation despite the detectives having nothing on him.

Now Black Ferris was in Flip's line of vision. Flip shook his head at the man's cowardice. His first instinct when he met Black Ferris through Ali was that he was a pussy. Black Ferris spoke more than necessary, and it was Flip's indication that Black Ferris wasn't as real as he was thought to be. Black Ferris thought everyone around him didn't have the heart to question his loyalty and character. Flip was surprised that Ali didn't see it. Black Ferris snitched, and he thought Flip was oblivious. When Flip called Black Ferris and told him he had severance pay for him, Black Ferris took the bait.

After checking his pistol for reassurance, Flip stepped out the car. He was en route to an abandoned home, a home where he was going to set up shop. The shop closed down before it started. Black Ferris was a glorified foot soldier, but he was still at the bottom of the food chain. When Flip called and told him he had that dough for him, it made Ferris Black a happy man.

Black Ferris was short. He was a borderline midget. His Napoleon complex made a lot of people shook, but there were those that knew better. The smile he flashed at Flip when he approached was phony. Flip gave him a phony one right back. The men went inside the home with Flip following him. Flip looked around for onlookers before stepping inside and closing the door.

"What it do, Black?" The men exchanged a handshake, and a brotherly embrace.

"Just stylin' and ridin' these young punks. Ready to run wit' the big dogs," Black Ferris said arrogantly. He was so dark that Flip could see only his teeth and eyes.

"True, true, but check it, you earned what I'm about to give you. Only niggas with big balls could run my shit. With that said, you got to guarantee that you'll die for my shit, and for what's yours," Flip said.

"Goes without saying Flip. I give you and my homies mad love, and I cause havoc to my enemies." Black Ferris was so convincing that he could have fooled Flip had Flip been less aware. Black Ferris didn't blink one time when he told that bold face lie.

"I want to believe you Black, but I can't," Flip said as he handed Black Ferris a brick of cash, and a piece of paper. Black Ferris wore a mask of confusion, and was so thrown off by Flip's response that he didn't read the paper, or count the money. It bothered Black Ferris that Flip would say such a thing, but he knew why. Black Ferris decided to probe.

"Talk to me bro. I could take constructive criticism, especially coming from you. Anything to get to the top," Black Ferris said nervously. Flip beckoned him to read what was on the paper.

Flip understood why Black Ferris had everyone fooled. The young man was cunning. Flip stared at the thug while Black Ferris read the letter, and shook his head. *And Ali vouched for this idiot,* Flip thought. After Black Ferris read the affidavit, he understood Flip's sketchy response.

"You don't got it in you to go to the top 'cause you a rat," Flip said, snatching the paper from him.

Black's instincts were on high alert. By the time Black Ferris reached for his gun, Flip was already on him. Flip rushed his space, grabbed his head, and rammed the twelve-inch blade through the back of his skull. He pulled it in and out a few times before Black dropped to the ground and expired. Thankful he didn't have to make any noise with his gun, Flip bent over and scooped up his cash, and the affidavit before heading out of the abandoned home.

Two hours later, Flip was on the road heading

east. He knew it would be a matter of time before Black's body started stinking up the neighborhood. Flip would be long gone by then. When Ali came to mind, he pulled over to the side of the road, scrolled through his contacts, and was thankful he was the only one that knew how and where to reach Ali. They had something in common; they were both fugitives. Misery always loved company.

...

After Tank handed a random pedestrian back his phone, Tank headed up Willow Street where he was to meet Claude. Tank had no choice. He didn't have anywhere to go, and anyone around him could catch a bullet by association. Tank still needed a weapon. He'd been blowing up the number Jewelz gave him, but no one answered. Tank was cautious, and had his guard held high. The prison bus made a late drop-off, and Tank been walking ever since the bus deposited him back onto the streets.

Tank didn't get the answers he needed from Claude, but he knew that Zane was kidnapped, and being used as a pawn. Enemies were lurking, and Tank's sixth sense was on overdrive. Tank needed to get out of the eyesight of those that could see the tag over his head. That dough could change a life. Tank resembled a winning lottery ticket on two legs.

Tank was a thousand yards away from the meeting spot. He concentrated on the thugs bopping up the street on the other side of it, but Tank didn't see the white Nissan Altima riding slowly at his rear. The thunder-like sound of a gunshot roared from the cannon of a Desert Eagle. Tank's body fell to the earth with a gaping hole in the middle of his forehead. Brain matter, blood, and other bodily fluids flew from his head like a Frisbee. Tank's soul escaped his body before it touched the ground. Screams, cries, and desperate pleas for help echoed in the vicinity. The driver of the Altima peeled off, and left tire tracks as the car's occupants made their abrupt exit. Seconds later, Claude and Lester pulled up, identified the body from the car, and drove away as the sound of the faint police sirens got louder. Tank's body lay lifeless in a massive pull of blood. When Fatboy and Jack saw the body from the Land Rover with their own guns on their waistlines, they cursed in disbelief. They had competition.

## 20

## Coral Harbour

## Los Angeles

The mood hadn't shifted since Claude's departure to Connecticut. Mark had to stop Sahara from giving Fatima a much-needed ass whooping. Now everyone was against Fatima, including her husband. Despite the beef, everyone sat silent in the living room while the kids remained clueless to the ordeal. They played without a care in the world while their mothers watched them. Destiny was placed on timeout for her disruptive behavior, which had been constant.

Mark stared at the screen of the laptop with intensity. He didn't know Tank personally, but everyone on Facebook offered their condolences. Tank's murder went viral minutes after his body was cut down. Mark knew Tank was with Claude when he robbed Calvin, and when Claude killed Twalique and Domino. Mark took his focus off the computer screen, and rolled a blunt to ease his anxiety. After licking the blunt back in place, something on the social site caught Mark's attention. When Mark clicked on Jupe's page, Jupe blasted Tank's murder, but one of the photos on Jupe's page fucked him up. As much as Mark loved Facebook, he was surprised that he never noticed a picture Jupe posted a year and half ago of Claude cutting the ribbon to the barbershop he opened. In a blinding rage, Mark swiped everything off the kitchen table. It caught the attention of the women, but they didn't question it. Sahara, on the other hand, went to see what the deal was. Sonya and Fatima remained seated on the couch stooped in their own fear and misery.

"What was that all about?" Sahara asked. Mark tapped Claude's name on his cell phone and called him. He beckoned Sahara to wait. The phone rang several times before Claude answered.

Mark said, "C, you never believe what the fuck I just found out."

Sahara watched Mark spill the beans to Claude on how Calvin may have found out his whereabouts which led to Zane's kidnapping, and Tommy and Tank's demise.

...

"Son of a bitch!" Detective Taft said thickly.

Detectives Taft and Rinaldi held their nose over decomposing flesh. Flies swarmed all over the corpse. The smell caught a lot of people's attention, and someone reported it. The fuzz identified the body based on the California State Identification card they found in the dead youth's pocket. Taft and Rinaldi made the connection immediately.

"Our informant laying dead in a probable stash house a week after dropping a dime on Flip. He's probably out of sight and out of mind. This stiff bastard probably had the link to Ali. Dammit!" Rinaldi said irately.

After covering up the body, Taft and Rinaldi walked back to the unmarked cruiser exchanging their frustrations.

# 21

## Wolcott and Hartford, CT

Jupe and Valerie's condo in Wolcott was sweet. Pictures of him and his fiancée adorned the walls of the living room. A smart television occupied the space above the fireplace. Hand carved crafts took some space on the coffee and end tables. The decorations didn't come from his mind. They came from his pregnant Italian fiancée. After splitting with Gloria, the mother of his two children, Jupe dated someone for over a year before she decided to go back to her abusive ex boyfriend. Depressed, shocked, and sad, Valerie sensed his vulnerabilities and broken heart. Valerie was Jupe's boss, and she liked him, but she didn't date coworkers and people underneath her job title. Valerie found herself gravitating towards him, and always looked forward to their conversations. Jupe never thought she was attracted to him, and he had mistaken her kindness. When Valerie accepted a more lucrative job offer at a different company, she left Jupe her number, and asked him to keep in touch. When he texted her a few weeks later to wish her the best, he didn't realize that it would turn into dating, lust, love, cohabitation, and impregnation.

Jupe received a call from Claude a half hour

ago, and Claude said he was in town to say goodbye to Tommy. When Claude told Jupe he wanted to check him before heading out of Connecticut, Jupe gave him the address. Claude seemed happy to speak to him, but something was off. Tommy was dead, and Jupe knew Tank ran with Claude. Jupe knew about the price tag over their heads. And now Jupe was trying to figure out what the fuck was going on, and what part of the equation he fit into. Jupe thanked the heavens above that Valerie was on vacation with her parents, and she wasn't due back until the middle of next week.

Jupe wondered if the police was looking for Claude, and if Claude was looking for somewhere to hide. Jupe theorized that with Tommy and Tank dead, there might be a war going on in the streets. Jupe still couldn't figure out what Claude would want with him at two in the morning besides catching up on good times.

The knock on the door paralyzed Jupe's next thought. He looked through the peephole and saw Claude and an older man standing alongside him. As soon as he opened the door, Claude's fist made Jupe's lights go out.

...

Jupe felt like Claude hit him with a ton of

bricks. When he opened his eyes, Claude and the older man stood over him stoned faced. Jupe had a bizarre look on his face. He moaned, grunted, and shifted on the floor before processing what was going on.

Jupe asked, "C man, what the fuck bro?!"

Claude had a hostile look on his face. He glared down at Jupe like he wanted to inflict more damage to him. Claude leered directly at the stone cold fear in Jupe's eyes before he broke the silence.

"I should be asking you the same thing," Claude said coldly.

Jupe said, "I...I...don't understand..."

"Les, make this motherfucker understand the damage he caused," Claude interrupted.

It didn't take Lester long to load what they were looking for on Facebook. When Jupe looked at the screenshot, he made the connection quickly. Jupe didn't know the intricate details, but Claude slipped out of town for a reason. Link, Domino, Twalique, and Ty played a huge role. Jupe indirectly exposed Claude to the world. The defeated look on Jupe's face revealed his guilt. Claude saw it, and he didn't like it. He kicked him brutally in the ribs. Jupe folded into a fetal position. Lester stopped Claude from launching another attack.

"Focus C," Lester said.

"I hear you Les, but he the reason why Tommy and Tank dead bro; cause of that fucking post!" Claude said thickly. The sting of Claude's words hurt. The shame and guilt Jupe felt outweighed the physical pain Claude caused him.

Lester beckoned Jupe to get off the floor. Jupe got up, staggered, and made his way to the couch. Lester placed the laptop on the coffee table, and in front of Jupe. Without uttering a word, he deleted the photo off his page.

"So you deleting the page will push Tommy and Tank out of their graves? Doesn't work that way bro," Claude said flatly.

"C man, what you tryin' to say?" Jupe had an idea of what Claude meant.

"That we, as in the three of us, may not come out of this war alive. You started this shit by posting that pic...now you going to help us end it," Claude said. Jupe felt stupid and remorseful, because it never dawned on him that Claude wasn't on any social media websites for good reason.

Before leaving the comfort of his home, Jupe took one last look at it, and he knew that the chances of never seeing Valerie again were high.

...

Deep within the bowels of inner city Hartford, Zane opened her swollen eye slowly. She heard shoes crushing the glass on the grimy floor. The light in the hallway was on. A large dark man blocked most of the light. The large mass made his way over to Zane slowly. One of Zane's eyes was swollen shut, and her shirt was ripped, exposing her breasts. They had bite marks all over them. Feces covered her body. Blood and mucus covered a small portion of her face. The grotesque sight of Zane made Calvin excited. He left her with no space as he came face to face with her.

"Well, well, well, if it isn't the infamous Zane. I heard you're a tough bitch, but too bad you're on a losing team. It's going to be a total waste blowing your brains out, but you and the rest of those cocksuckers robbed me. In another week, I'm going to make sure all y'all be good fertilizer for cemetery plots," Calvin said sinisterly.

Zane looked at Calvin with no fear.

"A week, huh? Claude ain't going to need more time to get at your fat, black nasty looking ass," Zane snarled. At that point, she wanted to die. Calvin kept his icy gaze, and he ran his beady eyes all over her.

Calvin said, "I'll give it to your dyke ass; you got

a lot of balls talking to me like that. If I didn't need you to get at Claude, you'd be a dead jasper."

Chester and Salazar's abrupt entrance in the basement halted Calvin's growing anger.

"Tank's dead, but his blood ain't on our hands," Salazar said. Calvin cut his eyes at him, and stared at his inferior intensely.

"Then you gotta move quicker than that. If my mom walked in here with Claude's head on a spike, she'd get a bonus. A price tag means it's free for all. First come, first serve," Calvin said. Calvin already caught wind of Tank's murder, and was prepared to pay out the reward. He had eyes everywhere.

Salazar allowed his stare to linger at Calvin. Salazar wasn't afraid of him, and would have driven a knife in his skull if Calvin weren't a made man with murderous staff members on his payroll. Salazar understood the killing game very well, but he didn't like Calvin's smug response. Salazar wasn't the one to have people read him. His subtle reaction sent Calvin a message. Calvin wasn't amused, and he didn't move his stare from his bold inferior.

"Salazar, if there is something you want to get off your chest, I suggest you do it now," Calvin said boldly.

Salazar maintained his gaze, but he wasn't stupid. Chester took note of Salazar's machismo, and he wondered why his body didn't hit the floor from being shot. Chester respected Salazar's heart. Chester was pissed that someone else beat them to their kill, especially someone that had a hand in his uncle's murder, but game was game, and they had to swallow it.

"I have no issue to get off my chest Mr. Calvin," Salazar said painfully.

Calvin said, "Exactly what I thought." Calvin shifted his attention back to Zane. The scowl on her face shot daggers at every motherfucker in the room. "I was gonna tell you that myself, but they beat me to the punch." Two of Calvin's bodyguards walked in on cue.

"And on that note, both of y'all get the fuck out," Calvin demanded.

Salazar and Chester looked at each other, and did what they were told. Outside of the price tags, the men banked off of Calvin. They carried a mutual feeling. They missed out on one hundred grand, and they both had it in them to kill the goons that cut Tank down.

Zane's tears blended in with the blood and mucus on her face. Calvin faced off with her again, and he snickered at the hurt in her eyes. Calvin walked away like he didn't have a care in the world. Zane almost spat in his face.

# 22

## Waterbury

At four in the morning, after tiptoeing past a sleeping residential assistant, Delores crept quietly down the staircase leading to the basement. She heard sensual moans as she got closer. Once she established a vantage point at the bottom of the staircase, Delores saw Kevin's shoulders hunching. His thin body was wedged between her pale doughy legs. Kevin grunted heavily as he gave the chubby, Polish client the fuck of her life. Delores steadied her IPhone and snapped multiple shots for concrete proof. From the sound of Kevin's voice, he climaxed into the patient. Delores saw just enough to know Kevin wasn't wearing a condom. Delores shook her head, and she sent the pictures she took to Lester's phone.

The following morning, Delores sat in the dayroom with some of the work release residents. She was a week into the halfway house. She was settled in. She did her chores, read books, circled jobs in the classified section, and kept to herself. Delores was still paranoid and edgy. Everyone was suspect, including one of her young, male peers that arrived yesterday. Whenever their eyes met, he kept the same gaze and facial feature. It was hard to read him. Either or,

Delores didn't like it. She was tempted to ask him what the fuck his problem was, but Delores didn't want to draw any attention to herself.

After closing her newspaper, the thin bald headed young man took a seat right next to her His mustache was thin, and his blunt demeanor spelled business. There was an over medicated man sitting on the opposite side of them. The young black male pulled out a small notepad, and wrote something on it. He ripped out the piece of paper, crumbled it up, dropped it on her lap, got up, and left the room. The man who sat across from her was still in his medication-induced stupor. When she unraveled the piece of paper, she read it. The guy wanted to talk.

Residents displayed rare smiles during the visit with their loved ones. Two residential assistants oversaw the activity, and made sure no one was passing contraband. They checked bags, visitor's lists to ensure accuracy, and maintained a safe environment. The resident's family made their stressed loved ones smile easily despite their predicament.

Delores and the guy who referred himself as Jay didn't have any visitors. They smoked their sticks while Delores's anxiety increased. It turned out that Jay didn't have a crush on her; he had information.

Delores took a pull of her cigarette.

"I remember when Alphonso was a baby. I came up with his mother, and she *just* passed away. It's a damn shame," she said sadly.

Lester told her Tank's involvement, and the news of his murder had her on the edge. She had no idea where Claude was. Delores was weary of Jay. She didn't trust this guy, but she needed to hear what he had stored in his head.

"I hear you, but check it, the info I got is worth some jewels," Jay said bluntly.

Delores asked, "So what's your angle?"

Jay died out his cigarette, and he lit up a fresh one. He shifted his gaze on his Newport.

"Ain't nobody fuckin' with me right now. My mom is on dope, and the rest of my people just caught up in their own shit. Its nothing personal, and I respect that. I have nothing. I need a come up. Once I get to where I need to be, I'm done," Jay said convincingly.

Delores looked at him closely. Jay knew Claude made off with a life-altering grip of cash, and Jay was doing nothing more than sniffing around it. Jay had vital information, and he was using it as a card.

"So what do you know?" Delores was getting

curious.

"That's for Claude to know."

Delores looked at him suspiciously.

She asked, "How do you know me? That's a lot of familiarity you stirring up."

Jay said, "You picked off Mookie and besides, staff leaves the census board anywhere."

"And what's your point?" She was getting agitated, and Jay sensed it. He didn't want to blow his play.

"Nothing bad Delores. From what I heard, Mookie was a problem to the wrong motherfuckers. You did a favor for the big faces and..."

"Fuck all this shit, Jay. I don't like your vibe, and I don't trust you. Claude ain't going to see you, but if it's about money, you got it. Get whatever it is off your chest." Delores had a angry look on her face. She was losing her patience.

Jay knew she wasn't going to bulge. He had to take a chance.

"Those tags over Claude and 'em heads is high. It's fair game. That shit is lucrative, and niggas is on it. I'm sure Claude would want to find them, and put them to sleep before they get Claude first. And with all due respect, you have to understand my point."

Anger crossed Delores face.

"Clearly Jay, but Claude may already know who killed Alphonso."

"I seriously doubt that," Jay said with confidence.

There was one thing she was always taught; never deny information whether it was credible or suspect. Delores could smell street all over him, and Jay knew that the missing information he claimed was solid could possibly cost him his life.

Despite her gut feeling that he may be on to something, Delores still didn't want to throw caution to the wind.

"Ill let you know something after dinner." Delores stood up and walked away. Jay watched her until she walked back inside the halfway house. He smiled and knew he had her, but his smile faded with the possibility of being wrong. His kids were down south, both of his brothers were locked up, he had no skills, work experience, and no foundation. Jay had nothing to lose except his fucked up life. Gambling was part of the game.

## 23

## Arcadia, Ohio/Brooklyn, NY

Automobiles whizzed past the rest stop on Interstate 80 in the early, cool morning hours. People were due to rise for work, and the truckers at the rest stop were preparing for another day of travel. A chubby trucker walked down the stairs of his rig, walked through some thick shrubbery, took a piss, and walked back to the truck. He started it and drove off. The couple in the SUV was oblivious to the departing truck. Peggy Sue Farley, a thin, pale brunette with stringy hair, rode the cock of Sterling Buck, a red headed burly man, in the backseat of his black suburban. The back of it rocked, and the windows were fogged while they moaned and grunted. After blowing a load of semen inside Peggy Sue, Sterling fell back into the seat and panted. He was exhausted. Peggy Sue unloosened the walls of her vagina after squeezing the remaining drops of semen from his rod. She rolled off, and sat herself next to him. Peggy Sue reached for her jeans, and pulled out a box of Marlboro Lights. She handed him a cigarette, and lit both of them.

"That was fucking awesome," she said sluggishly. She cracked the window for ventilation.

"Yeah." Sterling wiped his dick clean with an old paper towel, slipped his jeans on, and made sure his wallet was in his left back pocket. Realizing his wallet was there, and everything in its place, he put the wallet back in his back left pocket.

Peggy Sue peeped Sterling checking for his wallet. She figured if she needed his money, she would have lifted it from him by now. Peggy Sue just wanted a piece of her brother in-law's dick. Peggy Sue was one selfish bitch. Not one for confrontation, she brushed it aside.

"Is that all you ever say?" she asked jokingly.

Sterling said, "Yeah."

"Your such an asshole," she joked.

"And you're such a bitch," he countered.

"I told you that," she said in good nature.

"Yeah, you did."

After sharing a laugh, they quietly collected themselves. They watched the last trucker leave the rest stop.

"What time is it?" she asked.

Sterling said, "Its time for me to get home to the kids. They will be up in an hour, and the wife isn't due home until eight thirty."

Sterling knew he was wrong for cheating on his

wife with her sister. Peggy Sue was unkempt, haggardly, and she constantly scratched her hair. Her nipples were inverted, and her diet consisted of coffee, weed, prescription pills, and cigarettes.

After finishing her cigarette and flipping back on her dirty bra, Peggy Sue popped a pill and swallowed it dry. She hated her sister, and she didn't feel any remorse for fucking her husband. Peggy Sue's sister ruined two marriages and divided families. That was Peggy Sue's way of justifying her own amoral act.

Peggy Sue stepped out of the vehicle, followed by Sterling, but was greeted by a masked and gloved man holding a gun.

"Nobody make a move, nobody gets hurt. Run the money and keys," the man demanded calmly.

The woman handed over her pills, and the few bucks she had with no hesitation, but her lover had other ideas. Sterling felt he could take the guy. The masked man didn't see his victim's intent. Sterling sized the goon up with his beady eyes. He knew everything there was to know about weaponry, but it was worthless now. Sterling's gun was in the glove compartment, untouched and loaded. Sterling noticed the gun the thug held, and realized that the safety was still on.

Sterling made an attempt to humanize himself, begging and pleading for their lives, lulling the masked man in a false sense of security. When Sterling thought the time was right, he made his move with over confidence. He tried to disarm the attacker, but the masked man was quicker than Sterling thought. If Sterling were a nanosecond faster, the gun would have been on the ground. Sterling's attempt to disarm the henchmen was a failure because the gun never left the masked man's hand. Peggy Sue looked on with horror as she saw the masked man slip the gun off of safety. He pointed the gun in her lover's face, and he pulled the trigger. The traffic on the highway muffled the loud sound of the gunshot. Peggy Sue's screams were cut short with her own bullet. Blood spilled from her neck and mouth. Peggy Sue suffered for a few more seconds until she expired.

After dragging the bodies out of plain view, Flip cursed himself for cutting the pair down, but the guy reached for the gun he aimed at the couple with. Flip got rid of the .38, hopped in the truck, and sped off.

...

Ali and Raven sat in the living room watching a movie, but Ali wasn't into it. He had Percy locked into his mind. Ali had underestimated him. Ali was not at the top of anything, but Percy was smart, and he could hold his own; he had followers. Percy was careful, edgy, and paranoid. Percy was hardly ever alone. Ali sighed as he thought of his own cover almost being blown by allowing himself to get into the line of sight of one of Percy's followers. It didn't draw a lot of attention from them, but the dude got a good look at Ali's face, and that was a major breach.

Whenever Percy closed his eyes for the night at his woman's mini mansion, his armed goons were posted in the living room. The beef he had with the Dominicans was dormant after two of them chased Percy to a point where he ran over and killed a woman. Ali put two and two together, and he figured that explained Percy's paranoia and his heightened security. Percy would leave the state on a whim, and he wouldn't return for days. Ali knew how bad Raven wanted him dead, but his strategy to get at Percy was a dud. Ali thought of some rare angles, and they all carried the threat of death.

Aside from that, he missed his son. He didn't like thinking of him because it only derailed his focus in the present. Raven's wish was risky. He had no partner, lacked guns, and had no concrete plan. Thinking of his only child would only help increase his chances of getting killed.

"Are you okay baby?" Raven had noticed the grim look he had on his face the last two days. She asked him a question about what they were watching, and he didn't answer.

Ali was going to keep it real with her, but the second he opened his mouth, his cell phone vibrated. His facial features shifted when he picked up and heard the voice on the other end. He spoke to the caller for thirty seconds before ending the call. Raven was curious.

She asked, "Is everything alright?"

Ali knew Raven was probing, but Flip was an hour away, and he was looking for shelter. Ali knew from Flip's tone that he was in some shit. Ali made a note to himself to dispose of his throw away phone once Flip arrived. Ali had it long enough.

Ali asked, "You mind if my cousin come through? Nothing permanent. He is coming from Cali. He been on the road for five days."

Raven didn't seem too thrilled, but she nodded in agreement.

Ali knew Flip was hot; he could tell by the desperation in Flip's voice. He dreaded the idea of Flip's anticipated arrival, but with Percy looming, two heads were always better than one.

# 24

## Waterbury

*Zane had two handfuls of Josie's hair. Josie ate Zane's wet pussy like a pro. The Brazilian candy gripped Zane's large tits while pleasing her. She gave Zane's pussy a break, and climbed on top of her seductively. They held each other, and kissed like they hadn't seen each other in years. Josie's hand explored Zane's body as their tongues locked. Soft sensual moans escaped the pair. They felt the full effect from the Ecstasy. The women came several times from even the slightest touch.*

*Zane came for the fourth time. She wanted to taste Josie's tongue before she returned the favor. She rolled on top of Josie. Josie raised her own legs, rested them on top of Zane's shoulders, wrapped her arms around Zane, and she kissed Zane greedily. Zane's breasts were just above Josie's vagina as they grind from the intense pleasure. Josie leaked her juices on top of Zane's tits.*

*An hour later, the women were in a classic scissor position. They locked their right hands, and Zane wrapped her hand around Josie's calf for more feeling and enjoyment. The women were hot. They moaned and made animal noises as the thrusting* increased. They gyrated their pussies until Josie squirted. The sight of cum dripping out of Josie's pussy made Zane reach the biggest climax of the night. The women fell back and panted.

...

The naked women were cuddling, talking, and giggling. They were observing each other's body. Zane's thick cinnamon colored body turned Josie on. Her wide, brown areolas accentuated her large firm breasts. Josie was a light skinned Brazilian with a tan, and C cupped size perky breasts. Her nipples were dark and perfect, but the turn on for Zane was her eyelashes and waistline. Josie's navel was pierced, and Zane thought it was sexy.

After lighting and smoking a blunt, the women sat up. Josie's back was against the bed board. Zane rested in front of her.

Zane asked, "So you are not attracted to any male at all?"

"I'm strictly pussy. I think penises are gross, and would never want one of those inside of me," Josie said while circling Zane's nipple with her finger, and nibbling on her earlobe.

"What about you?" She kissed Zane softly on the cheek. "Do you like dick?"

Josie turned around completely, and now she was face to face with Zane. Zane rubbed Josie's cheek gently, and planted a small, passionate kiss.

"I don't have a desire to be with a man, but if I had to be with a male, it would be Claude."

Curiosity etched in Josie's face.

"Really? Isn't he in jail?" Josie asked.

Zane sighed. "Yeah."

Josie asked, "For how long?"

A pained look marred Zane's face. That was a touchy subject. Zane missed Claude. The thought of Claude wasting his life on a scumbag like Twalique angered her. Zane was enjoying herself, and she wasn't in the mood to talk about Claude and his incarceration.

"He got nine years left." Zane hoped her shortened answer would generate a hint.

"And he's the one that shot Twalique?" Josie asked.

Zane had an annoyed look on her face.

"Yes Josie," Zane said. Josie sensed Zane's irritability, but it didn't kill Josie's curiosity.

"I'm sorry honey." She kissed Zane on her shoulder. "But why Claude?"

"He always came through in the clutch. He never

*let me down."*

...

Zane kept her eyes fixed on the foyer, thinking about her past. She was alone, tied to a chair, bloodied, and beaten up. Her captures forced fed her, and they forced water down her throat to keep her alive. After that, Chester would provide a swift punch to the stomach, or a brutal smack to her face. Zane had a mustard seed of faith that Claude was going to create a miracle, but the chances weren't looking good. Five days passed since she was snatched. Time was running out, and Claude needed to make something happen. Chester was hell-bent on killing her.

## 25

## Waterbury

Fat Boy pulled up in the parking lot in the projects up Pearl Lake with all sorts of shit on his mind. He needed a come up, and he needed one quick. If, Fat Boy, along with Jack, would've made the hit on Tank, and collected the blood money, Fat Boy would have been on the first plane to Miami to start a new life. Despite having little to no skill, Fat Boy still wanted the American Dream. He wanted the finer things in life, and was willing to steal, deal, or kill to get to where he wanted to be.

Fat Boy pulled a Newport 100 from his pack, lit it, and exhaled. He was frustrated with himself. Fat Boy knew at heart that he'd never mount to anything if he didn't put forth the effort. He wasn't willing to do anything legal to obtain the life he dreamed. Fat Boy wasn't the brightest motherfucker in the world, and the probability of prison in his future was high.

He listened to a few more Meek Mill tracks before calling it a night. Fat Boy was notorious for sitting in the truck before going inside to face his nagging, obese baby mother. He fished for a roach clip in his ashtray, found a good sized one, lit it, and stepped out of his truck.

Fat Boy was only two feet away from the truck when his cell phone played his favorite Rick Ross cut. He snapped his teeth and answered the call.

"What?" Fat Boy was already starting to get annoyed, and he didn't even know what his baby mother wanted. The bitch was getting on Fat Boy's last nerve.

Sylvia said, "Nigga, don't what me. I'm hungry."

"What the fuck else is new?" Fat Boy asked sarcastically.

"Can you grab me a quarter pounder meal from McDonalds?" Sylvia asked innocently, despite her shit talk a minute ago.

"Goddammit Sylvia, why do you always do this shit? I just parked the truck. I asked you if you needed anything before I left, and you said no. What the fuck?" Fat Boy snapped.

"Watch your tone negro. You forgetting who pay the bills, and who's truck you just parked. Your narrow ass ain't no different then this kid of ours. Go get my shit." She hung up.

"Fuckin' fat bitch," Fat Boy snarled to himself before heading back to his truck. Sylvia was right though. His contribution to the household was little to none. Getting away from the bitch motivated his hunger for a better life. Fat Boy's son could always spend the summer with him if he gets the come up that he desperately wanted and needed. He hoped that he'd be the one to spill Claude and Zane's brains into the pavement. It wasn't anything personal. Fat Boy wanted a better life, and he would stop at nothing to get it.

Fat Boy got inside the truck still fuming about Sylvia's demands. She made him feel like shit, but Fat Boy had to take it. He couldn't afford to live on his own, not even with drug money. He brushed those thoughts to the side, and he focused on his status in society. He fired up the truck and tried to back out of the parking space, but someone pulled up, blocked him in, and wouldn't move. Fat Boy reached for and grabbed his pistol from under the seat. Instead of drawing attention by blowing the horn, Fat Boy stepped out of the vehicle. With the gun in his hand, he took two steps forward. Fat Boy looked left, and then he look right, but his motive was cut short by someone else's gun.

"What the fuck were you gonna do with that?" Claude asked. He had his Glock 9 buried in Fat Boy's cheek. The expression on Claude's face was unreadable, but the icy glare in Claude's eyes spoke volumes.

"What the fuck is this!?" Fat Boy asked incredulously.

Claude said, "You'll find out soon enough. Give me the gun...nice and easy."

Fat Boy followed Claude's instructions. Fat Boy didn't recognize the voice, and his mind scrambled. Claude frisked him once more before proceeding.

"Now walk slowly to the car," Claude demanded, poking the gun deeper into Fat Boy's flesh.

Fat Boy said, "Come on man, can we..."

Claude hit Fat Boy over the head with the gun he took from him.

"That's not what I asked you. Don't make me have to ask you again." Fat Boy knew that the guy meant business. Without hesitation, Fat Boy walked slowly to the car. He hoped to God that Sylvia was being nosy at the moment, but she wasn't. When they got to the car, Lester popped the trunk from the inside of the car, came out of the driver side of it, and lifted the hood. Fat Boy's eyes grew wide at the sight of his hogtied friend Jack. Fat Boy could tell that Jack didn't have a chance. Jack looked as if he was beaten and mauled by a bear. He was swollen, bloodied, both eyes shut, and soiled.

"If you try any funny shit, I'll kill you and this piece of shit," Claude said icily. Jack tried desperately to talk, but the thick duct tape prevented him from doing so.

After closing the trunk, Claude led Fat Boy at gunpoint into the car, and sat next to him with the gun trained at his face. Fat Boy stole a glance at his captor, and knew it was Claude. The person Fat Boy was going to kill for cash was holding him hostage. Fat Boy doubted if he'd see another day. Lester drove out of the projects unseen.

...

The ride was silent. Fat Boy knew he was a scumbag, but he didn't want to die. He prayed for a divine intervention, and as grimy as he was, Fat Boy felt he deserved to have another chance. He could almost feel death looming in the car. Fat Boy heard about Claude's hand in the disappearance of Domino and Twalique, and Link and Ty's death, and now he believed it to be true. The look in Claude's eyes and bearded face spelled murder. The ride was so silent that Fat Boy heard Jack grunting and making noise in the trunk. He closed his eyes, and he said a prayer without moving his lips.

## 26

## Greenwich, CT

Percy gazed at the clear night sky from the balcony of the mini mansion while holding a bottle of Hennessy. He took heavy swigs to escape the reality in his life outside of Sherry. His mind screamed with paranoia. The gunmen that pursued him were still after him. They wanted the money or Percy's life. His "not guilty" verdict pissed off the masses, but the Dominican dude he owed big money to was delighted. They had a right to be. Percy took three kilos off of consignment from him when he stayed in Miami. The guy thought it was the start of a beautiful arrangement. The Dominican took Percy's address, a photo, and his number in case Percy wanted to play funny. Percy had no intentions of burning him.

The stash house where the coke was being broken down was raided. Most of the cocaine was flushed down a toilet. Percy was left with no product and money. He contacted the connect, and told him the situation. The connect didn't give a fuck about mitigating factors. The connect wanted his money. The Dominicans were in Connecticut a month later, and tried to gun Percy down, but the chase ended in a woman's death. As of late, Percy felt as if someone was following him. Percy saw the short dude his cronies described with his own eyes. It could be just his paranoia, but Percy was going to keep his guard up. The Dominicans meant business, and they would spill blood from any kind of flesh associated with him.

Sherry stood from afar wearing a bathrobe, and obese-appropriate black lingerie. She saw her fiancé as a god and hero. Percy led her to believe that it wasn't about the money. He complimented her more times than her pompous parents, friends, and associates. Percy was amazing. She sucked his dick so much that she could taste it when not around him. The glow she experienced would not wither. She was on cloud nine.

Sherry's friends were in awe of her Prince Charming except Heather. Heather could smell through Percy's bullshit though, and she had been trying to break Sherry out of the spell to make her realize that he was only using her. Heather secretly wanted to fuck him, but Sherry would probably be under suicide watch if she were to find out.

While Percy stared at the sky wondering when the Dominicans were coming for him, Sherry walked slowly behind him, and she wrapped her doughy arms around his muscular waistline. Percy wasn't in the mood for that shit. He blew a short, subtle sigh of annoyance. He had to keep her happy so he could quietly seize and take control of her money and assets. When Percy thought of that joyful look she had on her face when she proposed to him, he nearly vomited. He couldn't see himself with her forever, but Percy couldn't see himself without her money.

Sherry became genuinely concerned. "Baby, what's wrong?" Her innocence pissed him off. If Sherry were a model with long hair cascading over her shoulders and a thin waist, the sincerity would have been received better. Percy had to put up a front.

"The whole world is against me Sherry. Just wondering who is in my corner. I've been burned and hurt so many times that I don't know how much more I could take." Percy could have won an Oscar. Sherry's eyes began to water followed by tears of love. Percy turned around and faced her. He didn't find her attractive the least bit. He knew he was fucked up for using her, but Sherry insisted.

"I'll always be in your corner no matter what. I've loved you since the first day I laid eyes on you." She kissed him despite the paranoid, funky mood he was in. After kissing him, Sherry sucked on his neck, chest, and moved her mouth to his meaty cock. Percy stood firm from his position and gripped her head. He pumped her mouth a few more times before exploding in it.

Percy never asked her for a dime. He didn't have to. Sherry showered him with unwanted attention, love, jewelry, and money. He needed to come up with a plan to ask her for that half million to keep the Dominicans off his ass. Percy had to treat the situation delicately. He was almost out of time.

# 27

## Waterbury

Lester slowed the car down to a crawl and stopped. Fat Boy kept his composure, but he was shitting bricks. Jack stopped kicking inside the trunk. The young boys knew what time it was. It was time for them to embrace the Grim Reaper.

Claude pulled Fat Boy out of the car with one hand. His other hand held the gun. Fat Boy had no clue of the location. It was wooded, dark, and the insect noises were loud. Lester popped the trunk and pulled the aggressive youth out of it. After removing the duct tape off of Jack's mouth, Jack seized the opportunity to plead his case.

"C, look man, we ain't kill Tank or Tommy! Y'all making a big mistake!" The look on Claude's face was cold and hostile. Jack's words went through one ear, and out the other. Instead of going for the beggar, Claude rested the barrel of the gun on Fat Boy's forehead. He took the gun off of safety.

"Y'all was still in the hunt bro. That makes you two cocksuckers just as guilty." Claude never took his eyes off of Jack. Fat Boy knew this was his last day on soil. He had to take another crack at staying alive.

"Real talk bro, I'm not going to beg. If y'all want

us to be guilty, then we guilty. We wanted to murk all y'all for the paper, nothing personal, but it wasn't us," Fat Boy said.

Claude took his focus off of Jack and stared at Fat Boy's beady eyes. It was hard to read the kid. Jack looked on feeling hopeless, silently praying for a miracle.

Claude asked, "Where the fuck is Zane?"

Fat Boy looked at Claude long and hard.

"If we knew where she was, we would have been there. This is all about the paper bro. I think you taking this too personal," Fat Boy said truthfully.

Claude stuck the gun in Fat Boy's mouth to shut him up. Jack was sure Claude was going to pull the trigger on his friend. Jack was more frightened than Fat Boy because he was hogtied. Jack felt useless and vulnerable. Jack expected his friend's brains to be shot out of his head at any given moment. Claude's phone going off in the car spared the men a few moments. When it stopped ringing, Lester's phone rang in his breast pocket. He acknowledged it and answered. Claude still had the gun in Fat Boy's mouth as Lester listened to the caller. After ending the call, Lester yanked Jack off the ground, and forced him back into the trunk before closing it shut.

"We gotta go," Lester said.

Claude didn't know who the caller was, but he followed Lester's lead. Lester was on to something.

After getting Fat Boy into the car at gunpoint, Claude closed the door and kept his eye on him.

Lester said, "It was your mother. Somebody want to speak to you face to face. Don't know how credible it is, but its information. At this point, anything is possible. Hold off on these niggas for now. Call Jupe and have him pick up your mother, and this dude that says he has information, and bring 'em back to his house."

Lester drove off with Claude in the backseat keeping his eye and gun on Fat Boy. There was so much going on that Claude didn't realize he would be seeing his mother for the first time in over a decade, but formalities would have to wait.

Fat Boy was relieved, but the night wasn't over. He wondered what stopped Claude and his boy from killing them both. Instead of playing a guessing game, Fat Boy went with the flow. Fat Boy maintained a little hope that they would come out of the hostage alive. He prayed that Jack wouldn't make anymore noise in the trunk. Fat Boy didn't want the men to be triggered.

## 28

## Waterbury/Coral Harbour

The residents were sound asleep except for Delores. Delores was fully dressed, and she just packed a shirt, jeans, and toiletries in a plastic grocery bag. She enclosed the phone charger before tying a knot on the bag. Delores was a little nervous about what she was about to do, but Kevin's transgression was an airtight blackmail.

Jay texted her and said that Kevin was in and getting tonight's shift report. She texted him back and instructed him to sit in the day hall. Ten minutes later, second shift were on their way home. Jay texted Delores back and told her that the coast was clear. She came down the stairs with her bag, met Jay at the staircase, and they both walked to the office that Kevin worked out of.

"It's a little too late to be dressed at this time. Y'all ain't now just coming in, right?" Delores and Jay turned around, and Kevin was right behind them. Delores put her overnight bag over her bag, and looked at Kevin.

"No, we are not just coming in. We are going out," Delores said easily. "We will be back before the start of first shift."

Kevin laughed.

"Look, tonight is not the night to play with me so I suggest y'all go to sleep and prep for another day. Good night," Kevin said before dismissing them.

Kevin walked in the office and shook his head. *Fucking criminals,* he thought. He locked his hands behind his head and sighed. Kevin came a long way. He'd been sober for ten years after hitting rock bottom. During Kevin's years of drug use, he lost dope money, his family, and his dignity. Now Kevin was king shit, and his arrogance was in full gear. He thought the world of himself. Kevin thought he was better than everyone else. He had a car, apartment, good weed, a few women, and his job. No one could tell him shit.

After Kevin did the headcount, he returned back to the office. Delores and Jay were still sitting in the day hall. They were acting strange, and Kevin couldn't put a finger on it. Kevin ignored them and went back in the office. His phone vibrated loudly on the desk. Kevin was going to ignore it for a second, but his phone vibrated again. Kevin figured it was the freak bitch that he met on a dating site. He smiled when he thought about the tit picture she sent to him. Kevin checked his phone anticipating seeing her tits again, but the video that was sent from an unknown caller had him stuck on stupid. It was a video of him fucking a client on the recovery side of the building. Kevin's livelihood flashed before his eyes. Now he knew why Delores was being demanding. Kevin opened the door and saw them both standing firm in front of the office.

"Which one of you maggot motherfuckers recorded me?" Kevin asked coldly. He was irate as fuck.

"I did," Delores said boldly. "And your going to do what the fuck we tell you to do. Now who's the maggot motherfucker?"

His eyes shot daggers at the pair. Jay kept quiet. Delores returned his icy gaze and grabbed her bag.

Delores said, "Turn the alarm off. And remember, there are more where those videos came from, so don't get it fucked up. If we get locked up on the strength of your mouth, your life will be automatically on the line. I hope I'm clear to you nigga."

Kevin wanted to spit in her face. He had to comply or suffer the consequences. Kevin knew if he lost his job he'd lose everything else. The thought of going back to zero scared the shit out of him.

He watched Delores and Jay walk out of the halfway house, and into the early morning hours. He stood in the dayroom feeling hostile, and looking stupid. Kevin played a dirty game and for once, it came back and bit him in the ass.

...

The tension in the house was thick. Sonya sought relief on the balcony overlooking the Atlantic Ocean. The moon provided a boost for the quiet tides. Everyone was asleep. Today was the worst day they all experienced since being forced under the same roof. Mark had to pull Sahara off of his wife because of the shit Fatima was talking. Since the incident, the house had been quiet.

Claude lightened Sonya's spirit the other day when he called, but he had been gone for a week. Claude's tone of voice seemed grim. She hoped to God that Claude was safe and would return. Tears of sadness, frustration, and love spilled down Sonya's face. The uncertainty was killing her.

Once Sonya came inside, she went to the bedroom, tucked Jasmin underneath the covers, washed up, and laid down. Sonya tried to exercise some faith in her husband. She couldn't help but to think of him until she drifted in a deep sleep.

# 29

## Brooklyn

Five hours after abandoning the stolen vehicle, Ali and Flip dropped Raven off, and decided to go somewhere close to have a drink. Ali knew from the fatigued look on Flip's face that he was running from something. Flip hadn't uttered a word besides giving Raven a simple social cue when Ali introduced them. Flip knew exactly who she was and wondered why Ali had her around. He was too tired to entertain it. Ali didn't press him about his abrupt arrival. Flip's story would unfold sooner or later.

The club was crowded. Ali and Flip made their way through the thick of sweaty, dancing bodies and strobe lights. They hurried to the two open bar stools before someone else seized the opportunity. A *Kendrick Lamar* song blared loudly as the heavy base seemed to make the club shake. The cousins got the bar stools just in time. Ali beckoned the bartender. While Ali waited for the drinks, Flip thought about the murders he committed in Ohio, and wondered if he wiped away all his fingerprints off the truck. He snapped out of it when Ali handed him his drink.

"Why you here Flip?" Ali asked, getting straight to the point.

Flip sipped his drink and looked at the dancing patrons on the crowded dance floor.

Flip said, "187."

Ali wasn't surprised.

"Somebody I know?" Ali asked.

Flip downed his drink, and got the attention of the petite, blond, blue-eyed bartender. She acknowledged him, made her way towards the men, and took their order. After the waitress left, Flip turned his attention to Ali, and looked at him flatly.

Flip said, "Yup."

"Who?" Before Flip got a chance to answer, the waitress came back with their drinks. Ali paid for them, and gave the waitress a tip. She thanked Ali, and the waitress walked away.

Flip and Ali downed their shots of whiskey. After Flip took a big swig of his beer, he returned his bleak gaze onto Ali.

"Your boy Ferris Black."

"What? What the fuck?" Ali was shocked.

Flip dug in his pocket and handed Ali the affidavit. Ali held his tongue and read it's content. His eyes widened when he read the name.

"Damn," was all Ali could say. Ali shook his head as he read the rest of the official document.

Flip said, "Damn is right. I had shit crackin' until that woman ass nigga started telling. Motherfuckers didn't have nothing on him."

Ali understood. He would have done the same thing. Ferris was his boy. Flip did what he had to do.

"So the pigs is onto you about that shit?" Ali asked.

"Not the murder. Just the shit that the faggot told the cops. He told them I formed the operation. I'm not going back to jail, fuck that." Flip downed the rest of his beer, and beckoned the same bartender for another another round.

"Anything else I should know?" Ali was hot and wanted to know if Flip's temperature was higher than his. Before Flip got a chance to answer, the bartender brought them more drinks. They clicked their shot glasses before swallowing the liquor.

After leaving the club, Flip ran it to him from start to finish. Ali understood the benefits of having Flip around, but Flip was hot. Killing a drug dealer was one thing; killing a white couple in cold blood was a different story. The other issue was Raven. She was uncomfortable around Flip already, and she wasn't thrilled by his presence. If Raven caught wind on why he sought Ali, there would be problems. Ali couldn't turn his back on his cousin. Flip wouldn't do that to him if the roles were reversed.

An hour later at the brownstone, Ali was lying next to Raven sound asleep. Flip took the couch downstairs. Raven didn't like Flip's aura. His sudden appearance was suspect. Raven had a bad feeling about him. The scar on Flip's face glistened when she stole a glance at him. She was disgusted by it, and it signified to her that his life was a war zone. When Ali pulled her coat on what he did to Aaron in *her* condo, the bad feelings went out the window. Aaron was their common enemy, and was on his way to put Sonya down for good. Flip threw a wrench in Aaron's plan, and put a permanent end to his motive. Ali diffused the potential tension that could have threw them all off course.

## 30

## Waterbury

Claude and Lester pulled up in the driveway of Jupe's home. The men surveyed their surrounding before pulling a bound Jack out of the trunk. Fat Boy was led at gunpoint to the front door. Jupe opened the door before the men walked in front of it. After letting them in, Claude saw his mother for the first time in over a decade. Tears spilled down her face. Despite the circumstances, she rushed her son and gave him a hug. Claude returned the gesture, but there was business to get down to. Time was of the essence.

"Ma, lets handle this shit, and we can catch up later," he said politely as he broke the embrace. Delores wiped her face with her shirt. Jay sat on the other side of the living room scared out of his fucking mind. He proposed the meeting with Claude; now Jay was shook and wouldn't mind rewinding time. The scowl on Claude's bearded face was intimidating. Claude's eyes looked intense. Jay hoped that he wouldn't become his victim.

After everyone got settled, Claude escorted Jay to the kitchen. Jay didn't know what to expect. He knew that Claude believed that everyone was a suspect. Jay expected the worst.

"I know you looking for bread bro, but I'm warning you; this information better be key or you going to be tied up like them niggas in the living room," Claude warned. Jay received the threat loud and clear. The threat made him lose confidence, but judging from the tied up goon, and the one held at gunpoint, Claude was on the verge of making a huge mistake.

"I think I know who killed Tank," Jay said quickly. Perspiration set in.

"There is a fine line between telling me something you think, and telling me something you know," Claude said smoothly. Claude wasn't in any mood to hear some shit he already knew. He had it in his mind to kill Jay. Calvin could have sent him to fish for whereabouts or other information. If that wasn't the case, Claude prayed that the slim man would have the information he needed to move on. Zane was held in bondage way too long, and the curtains were starting to close on her life.

Jay said, "I was locked up with Tank, and I knew his bunkie. He goes by the name Jewelz. I know him from Bridgeport."

Claude knew Jewelz. He was locked up with him years ago, and Claude never trusted him. He knew

Jewelz as a manipulator that had his hands in drugs and guns. That was his attribute in life. In his mind, Claude already knew where the conversation was going. Claude hoped that Jay was wrong.

"Those niggas were tight. Jewelz would refer to Tank as his little homie. He used to give Tank advice. They were inseparable. When Tommy got killed, it hit the jail like wildfire. Tank was fucked up over it. He confided in Jewelz. Tank ran him a war story that included him, Tommy, and three other niggas, and how y'all ran up in a made man's crib out in Southington and made off with money, jewelry, and drugs. Unfortunately, Tank picked the wrong story to tell. He didn't mention any names, but enough was said. Jewelz stunted like he didn't make a connection, and moved the conversation forward. And when that Puerto Rican chick got killed, Tank got paranoid because the consecutive deaths were too close to home. Tank said he was willing to buy the best weaponry he had, but Jewelz kept giving him the runaround. Jewelz left a few days later with Tank's math, and a promise to stay in touch."

Claude's head was spinning. He wondered what kind of angle Jay was coming at him with. Claude had to admit; Jay gave him some powerful information. If it was money Jay was looking for, then he got it. He cursed Tank about being so fucking stupid, even in death. Claude dug some more.

"So this shit your telling me; is it business or personal?" Claude asked.

"Both," Jay replied honestly. Claude was trying to find a chink in his armor. Despite dots being connected, Claude wasn't taking any chances.

"Why business?" Claude asked.

"I saw an opportunity, and I ran with it. If it wasn't for Tank telling Jewelz that war story, we wouldn't be in this kitchen talking," Jay said.

"So Tank didn't use any caution knowing you were in the next bunk?" Claude was getting frustrated with the late Tank.

Jay said, "Being invisible has its advantages. I did my bid in silence. I listen more than I talk. With that said, I got the drop on it. I'm handing it over to you."

Claude wondered how many other people Tank told. The robbery was so under the radar that it felt strange hearing it come from an outsider's mouth.

"Why is it personal?" Claude asked.

"Roscoe and J-Rock." Jay said grimly.

Claude's guard slipped a few notches. He hadn't

heard from J- Rock since their last conversation that went south a few years ago when Claude first touched Texas soil. While Claude remained in deep thought, Jay decided to capitalize.

"J-Rock used to say that you and Flip use to school him. Believe it or not, he gained a lot from y'all niggas," Jay said.

Jay was getting comfortable. He pulled out a box of Newport, took out a cigarette, lit it, and blew smoke out the small crack in Jupe's kitchen window.

"So why you know all this shit?" Claude's curiosity was driving him crazy and off course.

Jay said, "Because I was supposed to fuck wit' y'all cats on that heist, but I got locked up. My cousin Roscoe jumped in on the job in place of me. He was one of Calvin's bodyguards. It was better anyway because Roscoe was on the inside. He gained Calvin's trust. He was always around Calvin, even at his residence in Miami."

Gold was pouring out of Jay's mouth. Jay continued to prove to Claude that his information was solid. Claude let him go on without interruption. If Jay had access to Calvin's address, it would change the game drastically. There was something else he needed to know.

Claude asked, "So where the fuck is J-Rock?"

"Dead," Jay said bluntly.

The revelation caught Claude off guard. He didn't know anything of J-Rock's demise. Claude recalled the last conversation they had, and it ended in mutual disrespect. Tank's deceased crime partner, Ty, spilled the beans to Link; therefore, Link got a hold of Calvin and told on him and his team. Claude was under intense pressure, and he wasn't straight up with J-Rock. Hearing about his death made him feel guilty.

"What happened to J?" Claude asked, masking his guilt.

Jay said, "They found him in Mexico with his throat slit along with some Mexican bitch with a hole in her head. That's all Calvin bro." Jay grabbed an empty *Corona* bottle on the counter, and flicked ashes into it

Claude became suspicious, pulled out his gun, and pointed it at Jay. Claude had a glowering look on his face. Claude asked, "How the fuck did Calvin know J-Rock was in Mexico? You a man of opportunity, and out for that bread by any means. Did you tell Calvin where J-Rock hid?"

Jay wanted to piss on himself. He put his hands

up in submission. His confidence went out the window. Jay knew the jewel he dropped on Claude was airtight, and he didn't understand the gunplay. Fortunately, he had an answer.

"J.Rock's baby mother. A few days after they found him, she came up to see me. She told me some dudes ran up on her, buried the barrel of the gun on the side of her head, and demanded to know where J.Rock was. She had no choice. She feels guilty as fuck, but those dudes would have killed her." Jay was sweating, and his demeanor switched to fear.

Claude put his gun away reluctantly. He wasn't programmed to give a stranger total trust. He would just have to take Jay's word...for now.

Jay wanted to keep Claude off his ass. He added, "When they found Roscoe's body, Calvin's workers probed motherfuckers for more information on J-Rock. I spoke to Roscoe two weeks before he got killed. He had no idea where J-Rock was. Not a fucking clue. And that's when Calvin and his goons decided to take the drama to J-Rock's baby mother, and you know the rest."

"So what's good with that address? Do you know if Roscoe had a plug that could access that information?" Claude asked. Jay smiled despite just having a gun pointed at his face.

"I'm the plug."

# 31

## Waterbury

Lester's one bedroom pad was anything short of basic. In the living room, a nineteen-inch flat screen stood on top of a makeshift television stand. The men, along with Delores, had just arrived. Jack was out of his restraint, but the look on his face indicated he wasn't too happy about getting snatched and questioned. For Fat Boy, he didn't take anything personal. It was business as usual. He'd been held at gunpoint, shot, and stabbed in the past. He was numb to it all. Fat Boy felt that if he hung around Claude and his team, he'd be paid in full. He'd do anything to prove to Claude that he was a valuable asset. The opportunity was there to score big money, and Fat Boy was in for the long haul.

Claude had Jay call the sister of Roscoe. Luck shined on Claude's ass once again. Claude and Lester were going to transport Jay to Bridgeport so Jay could get Calvin's Florida based address off of Roscoe's GPS. Luckily, Roscoe's sister was currently using it, and she never removed the addresses Roscoe saved. That saved them a day. Lester could have Delores and Jay back in time at the start of first shift at the halfway house.

Claude, Lester, and Delores were in the kitchen

discussing something. Jupe stayed in the living room to keep a close watch on the outsiders. Jack quietly sized Jupe up, and he knew the man was forced into the game. Jack didn't like the idea of being snatched off the street, and forced into a suicide mission. Jack was tight-lipped and stewed, and he planned on contacting Calvin as soon as he was presented the opportunity.

The trio stepped out of the kitchen. Delores took a seat next to Jay. Lester took one glance at Jack, and knew he couldn't be trusted. Claude peeped it too. The stakes were high, and Claude wasn't taking any chances.

"Fat Boy, let me holla at you for a minute." Claude was confident he could sway Fat Boy, but he wasn't going to underestimate the kid. Claude read hardship in the young man, and he decided to probe Fat Boy a little more.

Without asking any stupid questions, Fat Boy followed Claude into the kitchen. Fat Boy didn't know what to expect.

Claude said, "I respect you bro. I think you a true street nigga that's all about that paper, but your boy gotta go. This shit Calvin got on us is personal, and we may not see tomorrow. I'm not trying to let that happen. When I pluck Calvin off the map, you could reap the awards as well. Don't be stupid. Don't let your nigga hold you back. If you want that turnaround in your life for the greater good, then you going to have to do some shit you ain't ever dreamed of doing to get to where you want to be. I see your potential. I just don't want it to go to waste."

Claude took full advantage of Fat Boy's youth. He saw something in Fat Boy, and he was willing to take a gamble on him. Claude hoped he didn't have to kill him.

Claude was literally asking him to eliminate his crime partner. In an instant, Fat Boy took a full evaluation of his life, and he knew it was nothing more than a pile of shit. The gamble was huge, and Fat Boy had only one shot of rolling the dice. Fat Boy thought about the American Dream so hard that it made his dick hard. On the other hand, they could all get killed fucking with Calvin. Fat Boy didn't mind going after big faces as long as the price was right. He had to make the biggest decision of his life.

"Understood." Fat Boy displayed no emotion.

"Good." Claude knew he was fucked up for putting Fat Boy up to the task. Having a good heart and trying to keep Zane alive wasn't a good mixture.

Claude had a good vibe about Fat Boy, but he had to test him. As far as he was concerned, Jack was just a pawn. Claude and Lester smelled revenge on him, and Jack needed to be handled. Before joining the group on the blueprint, Claude thought of someone. On the way over, Claude and Lester devised a strategy to get Zane out of bondage. The men acknowledged that they would be playing Russian Roulette with three bullets, and that they were outnumbered. However, Lester had more resources than Claude could imagine.

Claude was about to use one of his own. It was a last resort type of move he had in mind. They had to make a move now. Zane's life depended on it.

...

Ali and Flip have been silent since they left the club. They tailed Percy and his goons for three hours before following them to the club in Bridgeport. They were on I-95 at three in the morning. Flip didn't want to think of his own grime so he broke the silence.

Flip said, "That pussy is dangerous cuz."

Flip's timing surprised him. Ali twisted his face and asked, "What's that supposed to mean?"

"Exactly how it sounds. I understand her reason for wanting this nigga dead, but she got you planning a suicide mission. You do anything else for her?" Flip hoped Raven wouldn't be a liability. After all, she bailed from Los Angeles to New York without telling anyone.

Ali nodded while he kept his eyes on the road. Flip didn't have to ask any questions. Ali had been dangerous since the womb. Ali's deadly nature was enhanced, and his mind was caked with unrest. Ali was a walking time bomb. Flip was right behind him, and he had no right to judge Ali's motive. Flip was in the same boat. They were both fugitives. Flip taught Ali everything about hustling, and being the monster Ali was today. Ali was out of reach and Flip felt it. Flip had to utilize another angle.

"You said you been following this cat since you came out here. You didn't see any other niggas beside them three dudes we saw him with tonight?" Flip asked.

"Those are the only dudes. Other than that, I just know he using his big fat white bitch. She got paper...major paper. Mansion type of paper." Flip pondered Ali's statement.

Flip asked, "So its business too?"

"Yup. Percy ain't stupid though. Those three cats are with him at the mansion too. I'm figuring the dudes that were chasing him when he killed Raven's mom maybe still on his ass."

Flip opened his mouth to add his input, but his secondary phone buzzed on his waistline. Flip got nervous. Only a few people had the number to his burnout phone. Whenever he changed the number, he'd send off a group text with the new number to his chosen recipients. Flip checked the phone before answering it, and knew who it was by the area code 203.

"C! What up homie!" Flip was surprised. He hadn't spoken to Claude since he left Connecticut. Reality set in by Claude's tone. Flip knew Claude was going through some shit.

"You caught me at the perfect time my dude. I'm not that far from you." Flip's lips were pursed as he listened to Claude. Ali glanced over to see Flip's reaction to the caller. Ali hoped that no one from home was giving him a heads up about law enforcement tracking and closing in on them.

Flip said, "Say no more. I'm with my cousin… right…the more the merrier…favor for a favor… indeed…it's a long story C…text me the address… Stamford…see you tomorrow night…peace."

"Where we going tomorrow night?" Ali's curiosity was at its pinnacle.

"Waterbury. And yes, we putting in work. A favor for a favor bro," Flip said convincingly.

"Who's this dude?" Ali asked.

"One out of a few soldiers I fucked with when I did my dime in Connecticut. I put in work for him before we put Aaron in the dirt."

"I remember you telling me that." Ali knew his hands were going to be caked with more dirt, but he didn't give a fuck. Ali knew he would get something out of it.

Flip plugged in the GPS that he took from the couple he murdered, and punched in the Waterbury address Claude just texted to him.

## 32

### Waterbury

"Nigga is you crazy? Why the fuck should we run with these marked ass niggas? Them niggas is stacks of cash with feet bro. Nah, fuck that." Jack was livid from the kidnapping and the beating. Jack spoke with a thick tone, and he wasn't feeling Fat Boy's interest on joining Claude.

Fat Boy could honestly understand where Jack stood. Calvin had money, power, respect, and muscle. It was a suicide mission. Fat Boy thought about Claude's proposition, and his reputation since Claude hit the streets again a few years ago. Real always recognized real, and he couldn't disregard that.

Jack was talking major shit, and he had a right to. Jack swore on his dead cousin that he was going to kill Claude and that old man for scuffing, tying, and throwing them in the trunk. Fat Boy's mouth was sealed shut. Claude's proposition was morally debased, but Claude's reasoning of wanting Jack dead was solid. Jack proved to be a liability for Claude's team the second Lester rounded the corner after pulling off from Fat Boy's spot. Despite being roughed up, pistol whipped, held at gunpoint, and threatened, Fat Boy was wise enough to realize that Claude was only protecting himself and his people.

As Jack ran his mouth, Fat Boy was measuring both sides of the coin. Calvin's award was one hundred thousand dollars. One couldn't ask for a better come up. If Claude planned on picking off Calvin, the reward could be greater. If he decided to follow Jack's plan on killing all of them, Fat Boy would have to split that award with Jack. Fifty thousand dollars was a lot of money, but it could be gone a day or two after collecting it.

If Fat Boy decided to ride with Claude and kill Jack like he was told to do, but fail in the process, he'd be fucked. Fat Boy would get no money, and would live with the fact that he killed his crime partner for nothing. Fat Boy's mind was at a crossroads.

Fat Boy was placing another trash can liner in the garbage can. The piff him and Jack smoked enhanced his thinking. Fat Boy's trance was so deep that it took him a few seconds to notice that Jack had Calvin on the phone. Fat Boy gripped the garbage bag, and walked towards Jack.

"I got some info for you. That nigga Claude just dropped us off after keeping us tied up and threatened us with guns and shit. I know where he at..." Fat Boy had enough. That was the furthest he got before Fat

Boy wrapped the black trash can liner around his head, making Jack drop the phone. Calvin's gruff voice kept asking Jack if he was there. Fat Boy used every muscle in his body. Fat Boy's face looked intense, and a vein bulged out of his forehead as he twisted the lower part of the bag. The horrid look on Jack's face, and his gaping mouth were outlined on the trash bag. Fat Boy squeezed his face with the bag until Jack's body stopped functioning.

Fat Boy was out of breath. He had no idea when Sylvia and the baby were getting home. Fat Boy had to do something and quick. His eagerness to dispose of Jack's body outweighed regret. What was done was done. Fat Boy pulled out his cell phone and buzzed Claude.

...

Jupe knew something was going on in Fat Boy's home. Claude had him tail the men just in case his plan of turning Fat Boy against Jack didn't work. Jupe reported to Claude that they been in Fat Boy's home since they were dropped off hours ago.

It had been two hours since Lester left with Jack's body. Claude knew not to question Lester's resources. He just wanted him back safe and sound. Lester's constant coughing of blood concerned him, but Lester insisted it was nothing. During the meantime, Claude awaited Flip and his cousin's arrival. Flip called, and he stated that they are on their way. Fat Boy sat across the room finally comprehending his actions. He justified it plenty of times. It didn't stop Fat Boy from feeling guilty. Fat Boy was experiencing a void that he never experienced, and it started to eat him inside. Fat Boy didn't see the look on Jack's face because it was covered with a trash bag. Fat Boy felt that keeping the bag over Jack's head spared him the nightmares he would have gotten had he seen Jack's dying and pleading eyes. Claude sensed it, and felt a touch of regret. It was necessary, and it had to be done. Jack's potential to kill all of them because of his mouth, or by his own hand erased Claude's guilty feeling. However, he had to keep Fat Boy in line to make sure he stayed on track. Claude walked around the room, and took a seat next to him.

"You did what you had to do. Since you took the narrow road instead of the broad one, you going to realize that killing us would have caused you more harm than good. You would have to split fifty $g$ with that nigga. Fucking with us could net you way more than that chump change. I ain't making no promises on a jackpot, and we could all be plant food. But I'm coming for Calvin's throat and his jewels," Claude said with confidence.

Fat Boy nodded and took a deep breath. Claude knew he had the youth under his wing. Claude created a weapon. The young man passed the test with flying colors. Claude was going to school him some more until Jupe looked out the window and saw Claude's visitors pull up. Two men stepped out of the vehicle. The taller man had a pronounced scar on his face. The shorter one had a murderous look on his grill; the men didn't look friendly. Jupe mentally kicked himself in the head for accidentally exposing Claude, and his strong-armed, self-made success to the world. Jupe wouldn't be associating with men with murderous intentions.

Claude didn't acknowledge his phone because he knew it was his guests. Claude still held onto caution; he looked out the peephole for final validation. For the first time in days, Claude smiled at the closest friend he had in his life outside of Rocks.

"What it do Cali? Thought I'd never see your ugly ass again," Claude said, exchanging dap, a laugh, and a brotherly hug.

"If it wasn't for my shit storm, I wouldn't be standing here, but yeah, this is my cousin Ali. Ali, this is Claude," Flip said.

Claude and Ali dapped each other firmly and displayed mutual respect.

"Heard a lot about you homie. Much respect," Ali said seriously. Claude introduced him to Lester and they got down to business.

Fat Boy was young, and on his way to being a career criminal. He'd been around wide variations of criminality, but Fat Boy never been around the likes of Claude, and the two out of state goons. Fat Boy been around the typical fake thug that would never go over the top like the men in the room. Fat Boy knew at that point that the men were going to raise some hell. The young thug was thankful that he wasn't against them.

## 33

## Folsom, California

## California State Prison

After showing proper ID and walking through the metal detector, Octavia was ready for the visit. The sound of visitors, children, and correctional officers filled the air as the inmates awaited their loved ones. Two correctional officers watched the action from the bubble while a few of them posted in the waiting room to make sure no one was passing contraband. The trip took Octavia six hours, but it was worth it. She was bored, lonely, and depressed so she did an inmate search in the state of California. *Match, eHarmony,* and other dating sites landed her a threesome, chlamydia, and another failed attempt at her search for love.

Octavia entered and scanned the room until she saw her new love. Octavia smiled and walked toward her new man. The news she was about to share can get him out, or a modification in his sentence. It was Octavia's first visit, and she was nervous. She wore her best outfit, which was a pair of jeans, her son's LeBron James sneakers, and a red and black button down blouse. The weave Octavia had on her head looked like a rain forest. Moles and pimples stuck out of her make up. Octavia's blue contacts made her look like a demon. The more she smiled, the more Flex regretted putting her on the visiting list.

"Hi Flex," she said. When Octavia moved in to kiss him, he gave her his cheek. She felt like shit; she hid it well. Octavia knew she had to be patient with him.

"So what did you have to tell me?" Flex asked, cutting straight to the chase. She hadn't seen him since Raven's New Year's party. Flex trimmed down due to prison workouts, and his hair grew a few inches. Five big braids touched his back, and he wore thick stubble on his face.

"Well damn, how are you? Hope you are well," Octavia said sarcastically. She was beginning to sense that Flex was more interested in the information she harbored. Octavia didn't want to spill what she knew in a letter. She knew that the mail got checked when it arrived at the facility.

Flex smirked and knew he had to play his hand right. Octavia had the potential to be his outside line. His grandparents weren't in the best health to see him. They did, however, send money to his commissary every few months. Flex had been at *California State Prison* for two months after the judge handed him a twenty-five to life sentence for Trudy's murder, and his mother only visited him once.

Flex took one good look at Octavia and silently cringed. She wasn't attractive by any means, but he needed money, and an ear to the street. He was still unclear on Aaron' s murder despite ignoring Aaron's warning of a set up. That was the last conversation Flex had with him before Aaron was cut down by bullets. Flex was too busy looking at an unmarked cruiser in front of his grandparent's house. Flex had an idea Ali and Wade was behind the set up, but Flex needed and wanted more assurance.

Octavia looked at Flex, and she knew subconsciously that he deserved to treat her like slime. She fell for that reward shit, and Octavia snitched on Flex to a police dispatcher. That was something Octavia would never tell him.

"I'm sorry, you're right. My mind is fucked up, especially getting a twenty-five to life bid. I just don't know what to do anymore," Flex gamed. Octavia took the bait.

"Its ok. I could only imagine what you are going through," Octavia said gently. She rubbed Flex's hand, and to keep her closer, Flex allowed her to have her way. Flex looked around the visiting room to see if anyone was watching his exchange with the ugly bitch, but Octavia was the only plug he had. "I got some news that could probably cheer you up."

Flex disagreed with her to an extent. As far as he was concerned, his life was done. He didn't expect to see any kind of daylight anytime soon. It seemed like yesterday that he strangled Trudy to death. His time in captivity left him no choice but to deal with it. The crazed look she had on her face when he had his hands wrapped around her neck haunted him. The nightmares would often jolt him out of his sleep. Flex felt worthless, but he made the best of it.

"If you got it, spill it," he said blankly.

"What if I told you I know who ratted on you?" Octavia had his attention. Flex wiped his mouth with anticipation, and took a deep breath.

Flex asked, "Who?" He could barely contain himself.

Octavia smiled. She didn't notice the intense look in his eyes. If she didn't tell him at the moment, he may have reached over the table, and shook the information out of her.

"What are you going to do for me?" she asked seductively, hoping Flex could get a conjugal visit in the near future. Flex wasn't in the mood to fuck.

"Octavia, don't fuck with me. If you know some shit, drop it," Flex said through clenched teeth. She recognized her mistake, and she didn't want to lose him.

"Okay, okay, please don't be mad at me. Baby, Raven ratted you out. I read it in her text when I used her phone." Octavia knew she was telling a bold face lie. She lived with the guilt and ridicule of falling for an imaginary reward, and she hated Raven for planting the trap.

Flex wasn't stupid. He took what she said with a grain of salt. Flex needed more, and he couldn't allow her to leave without emptying every bit of information from her think tank. He regretted being oblivious to Aaron's warning during the last conversation he had with him before he was put to sleep.

"So how is that going to help me get out of here Octavia? I thought you had some real information for me." Flex knew her desperate ass was lonely. Her body language suggested she had something else up her sleeve.

She asked, "Have you been watching the news?"

"No, not really, but how is this relevant to what we are talking about?" Flex was getting pissed.

"You familiar with Ferris Black?" she asked.

Flex said, "Vaguely."

"That was Ali's boy. Ali put him on to Flip. Ferris talked a good game, but he..."

"This visit is a fuckin' dud. I appreciate you visiting me and all that shit, but I didn't plan to discuss a nigga I could care less about," Flex said thickly.

"Ali in New York," she said. She realized that keeping Flex in suspense was dangerous.

Flex asked, "You know this for sure?"

"Not really," Octavia said truthfully. "But I know Raven is in New York. Ferris said Ali told him cross-country, but didn't specify a state. New York is a hell of a guess."

Flex opened his mouth to say something, but Octavia wasn't finished.

"There's more," she said. "Flip is wanted in a double murder in Ohio, and I think the police at home caught wind of his possible hand in Ferris Black's murder."

Flex asked, "So?"

"I just figured you would want to know who was with Ali when they shot your cousin to death." Octavia's revelation stunned him. Flex hadn't heard Flip's name in years. Flex figured that might be the information Aaron gave him the night he was taken into custody. Aaron's warning had fell on deaf ears. Octavia had his undivided attention the more she spoke. Since Flex couldn't touch those responsible for Aaron's murder, he planned on ending their glory. If being a rat bastard could reduce his sentence, then it shall be.

## 34

## Brooklyn, NY/Waterbury, CT

The rain tickled the windshield of Raven's Acura as she sat in gridlocked traffic. The congested New York traffic didn't bother her because of the unrest situated in her mind. Raven missed her mother, and her patience was wearing thin. Raven wanted Percy dead yesterday. She acknowledged that it was an accident, but her mother's fatality created havoc on her emotional state. Raven was raised in the church, and she always believed vengeance was with the Lord, but Percy's acquittal made her go south with that belief.

Fifteen minutes later, she finally found a parking space outside her home. She got out of the car, looked both ways before crossing, and saw a young dark skinned man with dreads talking to police in front of her brownstone. Paranoia set in quick. Raven watched the interaction from a distance. The fuzz showed the man a photo, he shook his head no, and the police drilled him for five more minutes before they walked away. She gave the police a few minutes to get into the cruiser and depart before making moves to her residence. Fortunately, the kid was still outside. She took out a bundle of cash before seeing the concerned look he wore on his face. He beckoned her to follow him up the stairs and into the foyer. The news he was about to drop would flip her world upside down. It was money well spent though.

It was like *de ja vu*. Raven had left California abruptly so she could start a new life elsewhere. Raven moved with her mother to New York. A year after resettling, her mother was struck by a car and was killed. Raven brought her past from California, and now her past was creeping up on her. The police showed the young man a picture of Ali and Flip. She knew they were both wanted men in connection to murder, but who pointed the cops in her direction? It left her baffled. She tried to contact Ali, but his phone was going straight to voicemail. Her best bet for now was to get the fuck out of there and fast.

...

The circle of crooks listened as Lester ran over the remaining details of the plan. The men, including Flip and Ali, heard the plan numerous times since their arrival last night. It was 10:30pm, and Delores and Jay were due from their illegal departure from the half-way house in forty-five minutes. Claude stood next to Lester analyzing the body language of the occupants in the living room. Lester's plan was tight, but it could go south if everyone wasn't on the same page. Claude played close attention to Fat Boy, and found no reason to distrust him.

Claude felt bad about knocking Jupe out. After all, Jupe was unaware, and he wasn't cut out to get his hands dirty. The look on Jupe's face spelled fear and regret. Mistake or not, Jupe's fatal error led to tragic deaths. Claude didn't worry about Flip and his cousin. Flip proved himself multiple times, and it went without saying. Ali stood off to the side, and listened to Lester without blinking an eye. Despite Lester's sickly appearance, he looked seasoned, and ready for some action.

Claude couldn't stunt on Jay. If it weren't for him, Lester wouldn't be going over a blueprint. Delores task was to make sure Jay wasn't playing any funny business. Claude equipped his mother with a pistol in case Jay got funky.

"Jupe, go pick up Delores and Jay. Time is of the essence," Lester demanded. He and Claude used Lester's living room as the war room. They've been in it all day mapping and deep thinking Zane's rescue. When Jupe left, Flip chimed in.

Flip said, "I like it Les. Timing is indeed crucial though. Ali ready for war, but your boy that just left don't seem like he with it."

"He's not, Flip. He just doing the intangible shit like what he's doing now," Lester said and continued. "You and your cousin are wanted niggas. Your face is on the news, and I can't risk losing you. That would make the plan go to shit. Ali is going to Miami with us. You, Fat Boy, and Jay is going to handle business up here. We have hours to make it happen, not days."

Flip said, "I'm with it, old head. Zane is a cool chick. Just met her once, but impressions last forever. I'll draw blood over her just like before."

Claude felt that, and thanked the heavens that Flip never changed. He was the sole definition of a *g*.

"So when do y'all go to Miami?" Fat Boy asked. It was the first time he spoke since Lester finished laying down the plan.

Lester said, "As soon as Jupe come back with Jay and Claude's mom. The first part of the plan should be handled when we are en route to Miami."

An hour later, Jupe returned with Delores and Jay. Lester provided them a cliff note version of the plan. After that, the goons scattered away from Lester's house and proceeded with their plan of murder, kidnapping, and pure havoc.

# 35

## Bridgeport, CT

"I own a lot of property, shorty. I got enough stacks to set me up for an early retirement, but I live for this shit. I've been hustling since the playground, and my last bid can't correct that, so yeah, it's all about the paper. I breath, live, and die for this shit," Jewelz said arrogantly to Mia.

Jewelz spoke with an aura of confidence to conceal his insecurity of being obese. Mia, the fly light skinned chicken head he met at the club, wasn't impressed by his obesity, but the two bundles of cash he pulled out of his pocket when he showcased her at the gambling spot made her wet.

After climbing the stairs to her third floor apartment, Jewelz stood behind Mia breathing heavy. She noticed it, but she blocked it out by her own greed. She had three kids, and a fat sugar daddy didn't sound bad. Mia stripped in a sleazy strip club, and it barely touched her expenses. To the Facebook world, Mia was doing well. She wore furs, overpriced weaves, and posed for professional photography. In reality, she was washed up, lonely, and in dire need of a cash explosion.

Jewelz and Mia stepped foot into the apartment.

She placed a call in for an ounce of sour diesel since she was being treated. Jewelz wasted no time smothering her. She felt disgusted by his odor, but the thought of the fat man paying her way made her hot and horny. Jewelz felt her perky tits, and he slobbered on her neck. He ceased his movement once he heard the knock on the door.

"Your weed man must live around the block," Jewelz said in between kissing and sucking.

"That's right baby," Mia said, faking pleasure. "I never wait for my medicine."

Jewelz dick was so hard that he didn't want to let her go, but she politely resisted and he caught her drift. She adjusted her bra, walked to the door, and looked out the peephole. Her weed man had a blank look on her face. The second she opened the door, a man came into view and knocked out the weed man with the handle of a Glock 9. The other goon came from the opposite side and knocked the bitch out into the next world. Jewelz reached for the gun on his waist, but he grabbed a handful of air. He left his gun in the car. Jewelz thought at first Mia set him up, but after seeing her get smashed in the face with the gun, he knew for sure he was followed. Blood and spittle seeped out of her mouth while her body jerked wildly on the floor. The blow was brutal. The only thing Jewelz remembered before getting his head busted was the scar on the man's face.

The men dragged the unconscious bodies deeper into the apartment before closing and locking the door. Fat Boy hated collateral damage, but he had to knock the woman out. Fat Boy knew it would be a while before Jewelz woke up from his stupor. Flip could have killed him with the blow.

...

Jewelz slowly opened up his eyes with two human shapes in his line of vision. He never seen them, and had no idea why he was naked and hogtied to a beat up recliner. His eyes were wide, and they swept the living room. Mia and weed man lie dead on the floor with their throats slit, and blood pooling around their bodies. Jewelz eyes bulged with fear at the sight of the bloodied corpses. The man with the scar looked at him with psychotic eyes and a crazed smirk. Jewelz was no walk in the park, but it didn't stop him from pissing on himself. The fear he possessed was indescribable.

The other dude stood off to the side with a grim look on his face. Neither man looked recognizable. Jewelz did a lot of dirt, and he knew if he didn't talk or have the answer the men sought, he was a dead man.

Flip asked, "Now I'm going to ask you once, and only once; you familiar with Tank?"

Jewelz said, "Yea...yeah. He was my celly. Heard he got blasted."

Scarface looked at his counterpart, and beckoned him with a nod. Without hesitation, the dude pulled out his own blade, stepped to Jewelz, and sliced his gut with fluidity.

"Ugggghhh!" Scarface covered Jewelz mouth with his gloved hand to keep him from making anymore noise.

"We could do so much to you. Don't make us have a field day on your fat ass," Scarface said icily.

The crease in Jewelz forehead became more pronounced when Scarface grabbed him forcefully by his balls, pulled out Jewelz undersized dick, and placed a blade to it. The perspiration on Jewelz face increased. He knew he had to spit the truth. It wasn't worth losing his cock. But if he told the truth, he'd be on his way to his grave. Jewelz had to pick his poison. He decided quickly before the men reacted.

"I killed him bro, real talk. The tag was too hefty to resist, please man, understand my position. I could split it with y'all three ways, please bro, don't do this!"

Jewelz pleaded.

The silence seemed long. Scarface and his sidekick held a look of satisfaction. Jewelz felt bad for ratting on himself, but he was relieved. He kept it going since he already let the cat out of the bag.

"I did it myself. No partner. I didn't want to split 100k. Please man, just understand that it wasn't nothing personal, and it was all about the come up. Tank would have done the same thing. Can't sell guns forever," Jewelz said nervously.

Fat Boy was relieved. Claude blamed that on him. Fat Boy recorded every word that came out of Jewelz mouth. Jay was right after all. Flip had the look of a stone cold murderer plastered on his face.

"We can't all live forever either," Flip said before swiping his blade across Jewelz neck. The blade went in a half inch deep. Blood poured from the wound like running water from a faucet while he choked, gasped, and croaked with his eyes wide open. The men walked over the two remaining bodies and out the apartment as if nothing happened.

## 36

## Hialeah, Florida

"C, truth be told, I'm a little worried about your man. That dude been hacking, wheezing, and coughing since we left Connecticut. I just hope he won't be in the way," Ali said with concern. The men had been sitting at a rest stop for the past half hour waiting for Lester to come out of the bathroom. It was the early morning hours, and the trio had been traveling all day. Ali didn't express his concern out of respect, but he figured now would be a good time to voice it since Lester was in the bathroom.

Claude took the comment in and thought about it. Ali was right; Claude pondered the same thing, but he got used to Lester being around, and he relied on his resourceful mind.

"I hear you bro, but Les won't be a problem. Elite fighters have an elite trainer in their corner. A fighter would feel lost without him." Ali nodded.

Ali said, "True indeed. Can't argue that."

The men exchanged great dialogue all throughout the trip discussing the business at hand. Claude and Ali had a lot in common. Despite Ali's reservations about Lester's declining health, he enjoyed Lester. Lester's war stories were intense and real. Ali looked up to him, but the coughing and the frequent stops bothered him. Claude understood because it was the matter of life and death.

Something tagged at Claude's brain about Flip for years, and never had it in him to ask. Flip was his main man in the penal system, and Claude had enough respect for him not to intrude on his insecurity.

Claude said, "Ali, let me ask you something. Flip is my boy and..."

"The scar on his face?" Ali asked as if he read Claude's mind.

Claude nodded. "Yeah bro."

"Me and Flip is four years apart. I was still suckin' on a bottle when that shit happened to him," Ali said.

Ali went on to explain how another kid Flip's age at the time sliced him across the face. Claude was surprised that Flip received the stabbing when he was only six. Now he understood why Flip was so sensitive about the scar. Claude once saw Flip knock a man out cold for saying a subtle remark about it.

"That's crazy bro. Never knew that shit. Nigga had to go through his entire life with that shit on his face. Damn." Claude shook his head, and he genuinely felt for Flip.

"Its all good though. We made the nigga that did it stop breathing, especially after he killed my woman," Ali said nonchalantly.

Claude swallowed hard when Ali revealed the demon that plagued him. He could not imagine anything happening to Sonya, but Ali's revelation about his woman came to Claude as a reality check. In war, everything was fair game, and he knew Calvin had to die.

Ali told Claude about his cousin Colin being on top of Los Angeles until the same dude that sliced Flip's face forcefully pulled him to the bottom of the dirt.

Ali continued, "We working for this nigga. We making cash over fist, fucking lifestyle change cuz. The nigga pulled me out of a slump courtesy of the woman I'm with now. Then I found the chain dude lifted off my cousin after he killed him. At the same time, we still making those greenbacks, but since he and his team slaughtered ours, we planned on slaughtering his silently until we reclaim what was respectfully ours. When the dude went to Texas looking for some old pussy that left him, we started to put something together."

Ali went on to explain how they put a blueprint together for payback, but the dude caught wind of it, and the dude killed the mother of his only child as well as his best friend Wade. Ali admitted that Flip told him the drill about the dude, but Ali underestimated him. The more Ali spoke about him, the more familiarity struck Claude.

"About the chick he was gunning for in Texas, what was her name?" Claude asked. The pieces to the puzzle fell too perfectly, and he had to test him.

Ali placed his head between his hands and thought about the question. Claude watched him and waited for an answer.

Ali said, "Not sure cuz, but I know it start with an S. She's a nurse, and I know she bailed because he was kicking her ass...even raped her."

That was strange coming out of Ali's mouth. That was exactly what happened to Sonya. The woman Ali was describing could be anyone though, maybe a coincidence, but the description was close.

As the men waited, Ali was about to break up some weed until he thought of Aaron's ex-girlfriend's name.

"Sonya," Ali blurted.

The look Claude had on his face revealed all. It

was indeed a small world. All Claude could do was maintain a look of disbelief on his face. Ali displayed the same look of disbelief when Claude stated his experience with Aaron. Claude shared a story of the home invasion, restraint, and the ass whooping he and his cousin Mark inflicted on Aaron before sending him back to Texas badly touched, lumped up, and ripe for demise. Claude's cell phone jolted him out of his thought. It was Flip with confirmation. Phase one of the mission was in the bag.

Lester walked back to the car. He seemed a lot better now than he did before entering the rest stop. Daylight started to break. Claude and Ali told Lester about Flip's confirmation. Lester was pleased with phase one of the mission, but he'd be even better when Zane was safe.

## 37

## Brooklyn

## Waterbury

## Los Angeles

The taxi cab driver made good timing, but the traffic was heavy. It was 11pm. It didn't matter to Raven; she didn't want to go back to her brownstone. The detectives made their visit hours ago, and it was almost guaranteed that they'd be back. Ali and Flip were wanted men and she was sure someone was on watch. She left her place with no luggage to avoid suspicion.

Raven was on her way to go to the Bahamas. She finally got a hold of Ali, who was somewhere in Florida, and Raven served as the bearer of bad news. Raven had no idea who Claude Porter was, but she owed him a thank you.

...

Chester held his dick in his hand and released a stream of piss while having the phone between his cheek and his shoulder. He was in the back of the live tavern on East Farm Street. Chester could hear the echo of a *Kendrick Lamar* track. He was alone in the back of the club to avoid ear hustlers. Chester listened to the caller attentively; it was Calvin presenting him another opportunity for monetary gain. Calvin had received word from an unlikely source that Claude's mother was in the halfway house finishing her bid for the state of Connecticut. Chester smelled more money.

"You just made my night fam. I was just about to get up in some pussy before you called and dropped this jewel on me. Salazar know?" Chester asked with greed dripping out of his mouth while tucking his dick back in his pants. He wanted the big fish all to himself.

On the other line, Calvin smiled wickedly. Calvin knew the two greedy motherfuckers would light up the entire halfway house to find the woman that birthed Claude. Zane was a soft spot for Claude, but his mother was a different story.

Calvin said, "Yeah he does. Guess you have to beat him to the punch."

Chester was about to respond, but he thought he saw a shadowy figure looming around. He wrote it off and blamed it on the weed and alcohol.

Chester said, "Damn Cal, I'm buggin' bro. I thought someone..."

The black hooded person that he thought was a delusion closed in on him fast. Chester caught a glimpse of the sparkling blade before it was jammed repeatedly into his body. By the time he realized what was happening, his phone dropped to the ground. The thrusts to his torso and chest were lightening quick. His knees got weak, and they no longer supported his body. Once Chester hit the pavement, the thrusting continued until he stopped moving. Even when his soul departed from his body, the shell of it was mutilated some more for good measure before the black hooded assailant jogged away. It would be an hour before Chester's lifeless body was discovered.

...

The diner was quiet. Two waitresses were bussing tables, and a group of blue-collar workers were enjoying a meal after doing strenuous labor for long hours. Detectives Taft and Rinaldi sat in the corner of the diner over some coffee. The rumor was out there that *someone* knew Ali and Flip's whereabouts, but that wasn't concrete. They needed to talk to the source that put it out there before they decide on traveling outside the jurisdiction. Rinaldi had high hopes that the henchmen were in New York. However, Taft remained pessimistic. He felt that sending NYPD law enforcement to Raven's residence was a premature move. That error gave the fugitives time to run.

"Chances are, if Raven has any kind of current connection to those two fucks, they're long gone by now. When it was out there that they may be in NY, it should have been kept quiet and then they should have requested us to make the trip out there. Now I have a feeling we are wasting our fucking time," Taft said.

"Only one way to find out," Rinaldi said as he took a sip of his coffee. "We need to wheel and deal with our old friend Walter. The last time we pressed him about the Sullivan kid and the other murders, he kept his mouth shut, but I'll bet you that after being in prison for the last few years, he would be more than willing to answer some Peter Sullivan questions. I honestly have a feeling we're on to something."

Taft knew his partner had a point. The massacre that transpired a few years ago was an incomplete case. The only one that more than likely had a hand in the murders was Walter, and his lips were sealed. He only confessed to murdering Trudy Douglas and burying her. That was the only murder Walter confessed to. Police still didn't know if Trudy's murder was related to the multiple homicides.

"This asshole is going to want to play ball, and if that is going to happen, then let it be. But don't keep your hopes up. He is serving a twenty-five to life sentence, and the district attorney who prosecuted him is a real hard ass for a reason. Her own daughter was killed by the hands of her lover. And lets not forget Trudy's family. I don't think reducing Walter's sentence on a *Rule 35* motion would increase their faith in the justice system. And if he had a hand in the Peter Sullivan murder, I don't think he would be willing to incriminate himself." Rinaldi took a moment to process what Taft said.

Rinaldi said, "Unless he was granted a *proffer agreement.*"

Taft sighed.

"We are talking about murder in the first degree here, not a sentence for narcotics," Taft said.

"We need substantial assistance, Jack. Walter deserves to be at the bottom of the prison; yes, I know and I get that, but right now, politics and Peter Sullivan's family are reigning hard on our department and our authority are on us big time. That man knows what we want to know. If he tells us everything past and present, we kill two birds with one stone."

Taft knew Rinaldi was right. If Walter spilled the beans on Ali Ward and Terrence Rigg's possible whereabouts, and he was serving a life sentence, there was a possibility that he may spill the beans on the Sullivan case, and all the other murders. What did Walter have to lose?

The men sat in silence until they were done drinking their coffee. Detective Taft reflected on his own current standing in life. He needed to retire. His wife was hanging onto their marriage by a thread. Rinaldi had no life, was married to the homicide department, and yearned for a promotion. As of right now, Walter had the destiny of their careers in his hands. Something had to give. When the two detectives departed from the diner, they knew they had to come up with a serious game plan for Walter to speak. Detective Taft wondered how credible and how much pull Walter's attorney had. Taft heard some cocaine rumors about Walter's legal representation, but he heard Walter's attorney was good. Taft and Rinaldi hoped Walter's attorney was good enough to convince the DA of granting Walter a *Rule 35* motion equipped with a *proffer agreement.*

# 38

## Waterbury

*Darlene was living a good life a few years ago. She had a great man and a child with him who was currently in gifted programs and sports. Lloyd was everything any woman would want in a man. Lloyd was handsome, hardworking, and one hundred percent involved in his son's life. He was definitely marriage potential; he was an accountant, and many women wanted him. Women yearned to be with him. Most importantly, Lloyd loved Darlene. He loved her wholeheartedly. He loved Darlene like a man was supposed to love a woman. Lloyd treated Darlene like a pot of gold. However, Darlene had reservations regarding her relationship with him. Lloyd was too calm, collect, and educated for her taste. Darlene's urge to step out of the relationship grew immensely.*

*When Darlene heard through the grapevine that Claude was a year away from being released from prison, her panties got soaked. Darlene kept tabs on his release date through the inmate search on the Internet. She knew his movement in the system. Darlene somehow obtained an updated mug shot of Claude, and she was turned on by his size. Claude was rail thin when he first entered the prison system. Claude was* her first love. Despite changing course in her life when Claude got incarcerated, there was not a day gone by in fifteen years that she didn't think of him, even when she was birthing her first and only child. When Lloyd Sr. would have her legs wrapped around his shoulders giving her a decent fuck, she would orgasm thinking of Claude. Lloyd was aware of Darlene's past relationship with Claude; he made her cut all ties with him. Lloyd sometimes questioned it. Darlene would downplay it and label Claude as a criminal, loser, and an individual that would never mount to anything. Lloyd believed that for years.

The day finally came when Claude paroled. Darlene ran into Rocks, and he told her he was home. She got a babysitter because Lloyd was working late, bought an outfit, got her hair done, and made plans on hitting the club. She knew she was wrong, but she yearned for the moment the entire decade. Her vaginal fluids dripped when she saw and hugged him.

Darlene's plan was in full motion the day she sucked and fucked him. She wanted him so bad and all to herself. Claude was fresh out of prison and being backed up was an understatement. In conjunction with the sex, she gave Claude money. Her feelings for Claude escalated, but Claude had other ideas. He *didn't plan on making Darlene his wife. He secretly had a grudge against her because she bailed on him early in his sentence. When Claude was knee deep in the drug game, he quietly and slowly distanced himself from her. It drove Darlene crazy.*

*One cold November night, Darlene learned that Lloyd became hip to her affair with Claude. He called her a filthy bitch, she slapped him, and Lloyd slammed her on a coffee table. Later on that night at the club, Lloyd popped up, confronted Claude, and he got knocked out. Darlene tried to help her estranged baby father, but Zane, Mercedes, and Diamond stomped her out.*

*Her life started to go downhill after that incident at the club, and it began when she befriended Link and Domino. She smoked a blunt laced with cocaine with them, started fucking Link, and became his slave due to him getting her strung out on dope. She even told Link where Claude and Rocks were the night Twalique shot and killed Rocks. Zane found out through an unlikely source that Rocks' murder started with Darlene running her mouth. Zane retaliated by setting Darlene up to be ganged raped after fucking Darlene herself. After that traumatizing event in her life, along with losing her family and visitation rights to her son, she got bagged for credit card fraud and spent eighteen months in Niantic. During her stint in prison, instead of reflecting what went wrong in her life, Darlene harbored anger at herself for losing her family, career, being raped by strange men, and being a total loser. However, just like any inmate in a Connecticut prison, Darlene heard about the tag on those responsible for robbing Calvin King. She obtained Calvin's information by another inmate, and held his contact number close until she discharged to the halfway house. After she was admitted and her intake complete, Darlene made that call.*

...

At seven in the morning, Sara, an obese Caucasian resident with short brown hair woke up just in time for breakfast. She was a little bothered by the new intake's arm hanging off the top bunk bed, but Sara wasn't going to make a big deal out of it. She was hungry and ready to start a new day in her recovery. Sara been there for forty-five days, and things were looking good for her. Her obesity didn't bother her. When Sara was beyond frail, she was using. During that forty-five day stretch, she was offered the chance to relapse by the residents on the work release side of the halfway house. She turned it down, and that was huge for her. Nothing would stop Sara from seeing her children again.

Sara wasn't into making any new friends, but there was something about the woman on the top bunk bed that allowed her to open up. They had a long discussion before they went to sleep about how they were going to make things right when they discharge. She frowned at the horrid stench coming from above. It was normal to smell the farts of a roommate because the windows were locked to avoid people from going AWOL, but this stench was on another level. Sara figured Darlene must have eaten something that didn't agree with her body. Willing to prolong the friendship, Sara attempted to wake the woman up by tugging on her new friend's arm. When Sara didn't get a response, she got suspicious. She got up out of her bed, took one look at Darlene, and screamed at the top of her lungs. Sara's screaming woke the other residents. A few residential assistants charged into the room. Kevin, from the work release side, came in the room a few seconds later because he was done with his shift and on his way out. Other residents tried to be nosy, but they were redirected away from the room. The morning staff knew that the day would be filled with questioning, paperwork, and police, for Darlene's opened eye lifeless body leaked bodily fluids all over the top bunk. The dope needle next to her corpse was the cause of her demise.

## 39

## Miami

The snooty, lush and green neighborhood where Calvin's residence was located was a few miles away from the beach. The three men that sat outside Calvin's spot witnessed little activity. Claude and Ali were growing impatient and restless because time was dwindling. Two of Calvin's workers were in and out since the three arrived. One of them was a caramel colored muscular man whose arms were loaded with tattoos. The other dark skinned goon had a slim build with a Mohawk. Lester sat in the passenger seat of the sedan holding binoculars.

"The next opening that pop up, we in there," Claude spat.

"I hear you cuz. Sitting in this rich shit is a little hot," Ali said nervously. He had been shaken up since Raven called and told him that the police came to her brownstone asking questions. His paranoia was at its pinnacle.

Lester kept the binoculars steady on his face. The only way Claude and Ali would notice any activity was if they took turns with the binoculars. Lester shifted as he noticed the woman of Calvin's life.

"Oh shit, what's this?" Lester asked as he looked

on trying to gather what was happening before his eyes. The moment that the men were seeking had arrived. Lester gave the binoculars to Claude to see if the Oriental woman looked familiar to him. She arrived at the house with a Hispanic man and a toddler. The two other henchmen met them outside the residence. Claude had to get his adrenaline under control. He recognized her at first glance. Ali pulled out his share of the weaponry and handed a gun to Claude. It was perfect timing. The two goons that were in and out of the swank residence got inside a black Denali and left leaving Calvin's wife, the Hispanic, and the toddler. Lester thought of something, and he was sure Claude and Ali thought the same thing.

"He's fucking her," Claude said.

The last thing Claude wanted to do was involve an innocent child, but Claude didn't plan on playing by any rules since his own family was at risk for a slaughter.

"We still have to wait fellas. There could be more motherfuckers in the house with more fuckers coming. Patience will only keep us and Zane alive. We'll wait until it gets dark when they are settled in. If my instinct serves me correct, those dudes won't come back. That bitch may be in charge since Calvin ain't down here," Lester said.

Claude and Ali reluctantly agreed, placed their
weapons at their side, and remained put. A few hours
later, they made their move. Lester stayed in the car
and remained on watch.

...

Calvin's home was nothing short of excellent.
His Spaniard style residence had a wrought-iron gate
around it. The house had stucco walls and a red-tiled
roof. The sprinkling system nourished the sprawling
lawn every fifteen minutes. The only problem about
the home was the two men who made it over the gate
unnoticed. Lester theorized before the sun went down
that if Calvin's wife and the worker were fucking, the
security system would more than likely be shut down.

...

Jessica King rode Juan Rio's cock like a
professional while he played with her tits. It was the
best pussy Juan ever had. He fell in love with her four
days after Calvin left for Connecticut. Juan wanted her
to be the lady of his life. When Jessica first started
flirting, Juan avoided eye contact, and he didn't want
to get in the crosshair of Calvin's gun. Juan feared
Calvin just like a Christian fears God. Now it was
different. He wanted to kill Calvin. Jessica's pussy

corrupted the shit out of him, and it made him throw caution into the wind. Jessica secretly wanted him dead as well. Calvin had a huge life insurance policy and a will promising her everything that a woman needed and wanted. The pair wouldn't mind cashing in on the will and life insurance policy. The idea started off as a joke, but a day later, it turned into premeditation. Juan had been fucking her for four days, and they were already scheming on his wealth. Jessica justified it by the jealousy, insecurity, and beatings. Juan justified it by Calvin's harsh treatment of him.

After riding his dick, Jessica sucked it good and hard. Juan had his mouth open, steeped in passion. He gripped Jessica's long hair and pumped her mouth. He didn't realize her throat was that deep.

"Uh...yeah," Juan blurted smoothly.

Slurping noises filled the master bedroom. Jessica sucked him off fast and slow before Juan positioned his body on top of hers. Juan slid his unprotected dick into her and deep stroked her. She made animal noises and other sensual sounds before coming to her climax. On cue, Juan shot the biggest load in his life inside of her. He remained on top of her exhausted, and feeling an adrenaline rush because he fucked the wife of his boss, but it was well worth the sexual exercise.

"That was fantastic," Jessica said sensually.

"Yes it was," Juan said. He was still panting. He gave it to her good.

"How many times did you cum?" Juan was curious. He was pretty sure that his fat fuck of a boss never lasted ten minutes. He figured his dick game was tight.

"I came several times baby. I am capable of having multiple orgasms. You've exceeded all of my expectations. You're a keeper," Jessica said as she winked her eye.

Juan got off of her and rolled to Calvin's side of the bed. There was a question that swirled in his head since he started working for Calvin, and now he felt that the time was right to ask.

Juan asked, "What do you see in him? You have the look of an America's top model despite being Asian. I know Calvin is a made man, but he is one ugly bastard. I'm just saying."

Jessica looked at him and smiled. "I'm sure you know the answer to that so I'm not going to answer, but believe it or not, he has some qualities. He's caring, charming, and is a great father to Sayo. She adores him. I can't take that away from him."

Juan nodded.

"So it took him two minutes to create your daughter?" Juan asked, trying to be funny.

"Oh stop," Jessica said. "He wasn't that bad. It took him five." They both laughed. Juan looked around and was amazed of what Calvin had done for himself and his family. The Jacuzzi in their bathroom was enough to fit four people in it. Calvin had three safes in his bedroom, and he showered Jessica with jewelry from different countries. Juan spotted three *Rolex* watches, two *Cartier* rings, and two *Louis Vuitton* watches on the dresser alone. He could only imagine what was in the safes. If Juan weren't afraid of Calvin, he would take them. He peeped the walk-in closet that was the size of a kid's room. There were over a million dollars worth of Calvin and Jessica's clothes, shoes, and jewelry. In all the years he worked for Calvin, he never been inside the master bedroom. It was another world. The rest of Calvin's upscale house was spectacular. An oil-stained portrait of Calvin and Jessica covered the wall on top of the fireplace downstairs. A sweeping staircase added another notch of delicacy in the home. The more he took in Calvin's lavish place, the more comfortable he became at

Jessica's idea of pushing Calvin off the planet for his life insurance policy.

Juan asked, "So Jess, how do you want your husband's life to end? Bullets? Poison? I say undetectable poison. There is no better way than that. We may need a whole lot of it to end the fat fuck's life."

Jessica smiled wickedly. "Sounds good to me as long as it's undetectable. Forensics can land us both in a cage."

Juan was about to say something, but Jessica's child knocked safely on the door. Jessica panicked because Sayo had the potential to climb out of her crib; she'd witnessed it herself. Juan sprinted to the bathroom to avoid being seen. She put her robe on to cover her naked body, walked to the door and opened it. She recoiled from the shock. Two unfamiliar men stood at her bedroom door. The stockier one held her only child. Sayo was asleep on his shoulder. The smaller goon had a scowl on his face. Jessica was scared to death and uncertain of the men's motives. Jessica kicked herself for sending Calvin's workers away from the premises so she could get her fuck on. She slipped badly. If she remembered to turn on the alarm system, the men would not be standing in front of her. Jessica wondered if Calvin hired the thugs to spy.

"Who are you and what are you doing in my house? I could have the both of you arrested," Jessica said sharply.

The intruders looked at each other and smiled.

"Come out the bathroom pussy, and I want those hands in the air," Claude demanded.

"Look, if money is what you want, please feel free to indulge," Jessica pleaded. The cop threat posed no deterrent to the men.

Juan walked slowly out of the bathroom with Calvin's robe on his naked body. Ali beckoned him with his gun to sit down. Juan sat slowly with his hands still in the air.

Claude said, "That would be ideal, but that's secondary. The first thing we want you to do is to call your husband on *Tango*. If you don't have it on your phone, install that shit now. When all is said and done, then you can hand us those jewels and greenbacks."

Jessica finally knew who that man was. She didn't know him by name, but she recognized the voice from the first robbery that happened in Greenwich, Connecticut. She didn't have to install *Tango* because it was already on her phone, but she had to think fast.

Jessica said, "Instead of doing that, can I hand you everything you need..."

"Bitch, I don't care if you fuckin' this motherfucker behind Calvin's back. Personally, I don't blame you. But you just made our plan a lot easier, and he's going to know whether you like it or not," Claude responded.

Ali had the gun trained on Juan and watched him like a hawk, even though he could see both of his hands. Ali didn't want to shove caution to the side. His mind could have wondered somewhere else, but lives were on the line, and he didn't want to take any unnecessary chances. While watching Calvin's house from a distance a few hours ago, Ali already planned to take Raven and leave the country.

"Please papi, he's going to kill us both," Juan said cowardly.

"Not our problem," Claude spat. "You should have thought about that before you fucked her."

Claude shifted the attention to Jessica.

"Make that *Tango* call. I'm not going to ask you again," Claude said evenly.

Tears spilled down Jessica's face out of fear, not regret. She knew for sure that if the men didn't kill her, Calvin would. Ali took the baby from Claude, and positioned the pair together on the bed so Calvin could get a full view. Jessica and Juan hoped that Calvin was unavailable. Both of them gasped when he picked up. They smelled their own death.

## 40

## Hartford

Zane heard Calvin's shoes click-clacking on the debris ridden floor. She had been bound for days, and she was able to tell the difference between Calvin, Chester, and Salazar's footsteps. The abuse the men inflicted on her subsided, and her left eye opened after being swollen shut for three and a half days. Her psyche was growing dim and unpleasant. Chester stopped attacking her because she was numb to it. Zane started to embrace her pending death. She admitted to herself that her faith in Claude was lost. Zane was at peace and wasn't mad at him. She knew deep within the root of her heart that Claude tried, and he was valiant in his effort to save her. He probably died trying.

The basement was dark, murky, and smelled like shit. Zane was an uncontrollable mess. She was covered in feces, blood, and vomit. Her captors fed her little, but they gave her water to keep her alive. When Calvin entered the basement, he didn't look too happy. But what else was new? The snarl seemed stuck on his face. Salazar was at his rear. She kept her eyes closed, but she heard them clearly.

"I don't know full detail, but Chester die. He got

stabbed. Don't know who. I just know he die," Salazar said.

Calvin dug in the breast pocket of his suit and pulled out a *Louixs* and lit it. He looked at Zane coldly before blowing cigar smoke in her direction.

"I think it's about time we kill this bitch. With her dead, I'll call it even," Calvin said. Calvin's advisor's words started to click. Calvin just wanted Claude to feel some deeply rooted grievance. Calvin wanted Claude to regret strong-arming his paper and jewels in front of his family. Calvin would rather have Claude's head in a Stop and Shop bag, but Zane would have to do. It was too bad to pick off a cute dyke, but Claude earned it. Even with being covered with blood, shit, and vomit, she was still one sexy bitch.

Calvin said, "Take her somewhere and kill her. When you're done, you can collect the whole prize now that Chester is a memory." Calvin bit the end of his cigar off and lit it. "So you have no idea on what happened to that motherfucker?"

Salazar shook his head.

"Not even a hint."

Calvin had a feeling Chester's death came from the same hands that wanted to kill him. Chester's death was a mystery to him. Salazar had a difficult time containing his excitement. He respected Zane and her machisma, but it would be an easy kill for him. Salazar could care less about Chester's death; he felt it was God's blessing. Zane heard their conversation, and a new stream of fear invaded her. Now she was desperate to live. She wanted Claude to bust right through the basement door and save her. The realization set in quick.

Once Calvin beckoned Salazar to do the honors of cutting her throat, Salazar walked to Zane holding his favorite blade. It was the blade that ended many lives. Zane's life flashed before her eyes when Salazar approached her. She fearfully embraced it. Instead of Claude making a heroic grand entrance, Calvin's phone buzzed.

Calvin delayed Salazar's murderous intentions when he saw that it was his wife calling him. Calvin found it usual because she was calling using *Tango* video. He expected to see his wife. Instead, he saw Claude in his bedroom holding his only offspring. Calvin's breathing became unmanageable, and panic exploded in his heart. He put his cigar out, dug out his inhaler, and supplied himself with a double dose. Calvin got his air supply back, but he was still speechless. Claude rocked his sleeping daughter gently. The only silver lining he saw was that Sayo was still alive, but where was his wife? Where the fuck were his men? Claude broke the ice before Calvin had a chance to bombard him with questions.

"Calvin King, how are you? I didn't know a fat bastard like yourself could produce something so precious." Claude kissed Sayo softly on the cheek as if she was his child.

"You motherfucking cocksocker! You hurt my baby and I'll kill your whole fucking family!" Calvin said thickly.

Calvin's heart raced a mile per second. The initial shock of witnessing Claude being in his house was indescribable, but to see his child slumped over his adversary's shoulder was the meat and potatoes. The smirk Claude wore was the cheery on top. Calvin knew Claude was enjoying it. Calvin reflected on what his advisor told him in the beginning of the week. He warned Calvin. The advisor told Calvin he should have taken the loss on the chin. Now the game changed by a simple shift of the wind.

Salazar looked on quietly. He didn't give a fuck about Calvin's family; he wanted his money. Salazar knew he wasn't collecting any reward anytime soon.

While Claude witnessed Calvin self-destruct, he

was ready to add some seasoning. He removed himself from the video and rotated it around the room, capturing Ali. Calvin had no idea who that was. He expected to see Jessica hogtied, but what he saw next froze him.

"Cat got your tongue capo? Kings always lack the caution of a common man," Claude said. Calvin was going to kill them both for their betrayal. Juan too was in his bedroom wearing Calvin's favorite robe. Jessica wore her own robe until Ali slowly disrobed her at Claude's request, exposing her slim body and perky tits.

Claude said, "And you want to hear some more raw truth? Me and my man right here stood outside your door for a good half hour before making our presence known with your baby. She sent your other workers home and killed the alarm system. Your hired help was fucking the shit out of your wife and she *loved* it."

"You a goddamned lie! Y'all staged this shit!" Calvin blasted.

Claude and Ali laughed.

"Think how you want to think. When you come down here with Zane, I'll prove it to you. These smart phones can capture noise in any background, especially dialogue. Your worker and your bitch want that life insurance paper you got. I heard you *just* got it," Claude said jokingly.

Calvin clung onto every single word that came out of Claude's mouth. His mind was spinning, and he did just get life insurance. He would have no choice but to kill his wife and her lover because they had a hit on him anyway. For every pawn Calvin eliminated, Claude came right back and matched him. Jewelz had that paper Calvin gave him for two days before Claude had him bumped. It was a waste of money.

"So Cal, we could produce bloodshed or make peace. All I want is Zane," Claude said.

Calvin knew he was a king on the chessboard and was being check mated. Despite how he felt, he had to swallow his pride and comply.

"On our way," Calvin said dejectedly. Claude nodded before responding.

"No funny shit bro. We ain't the only ones down here. Anybody that come on your property is getting clipped," Claude threatened.

The phone line disconnected after the threat. Calvin stood still for a second looking dumbfounded. He wanted to shoot himself in the head for underestimating Claude. As a result of his own stupidity, his family was in grave danger.

"Untie the bitch Sal and clean her up. We heading out," Calvin said. Salazar's hope of getting that grip faded. He felt that it would be bad timing to inquire about it now.

## 41

## Coral Harbour

Mark, Sahara, Fatima, and the bodyguard dropped Raven off at the house before going shopping for food. They had just picked her up from the airport. Raven had been shaken up by the recent turn of events, and she finally realized that justice for her mother's accidental death would have to wait. Ali was hot. Flip's arrival made him even hotter and she had ties to both of them. When she dropped the bomb on Ali about detectives asking questions, he didn't reveal his location, which was a good thing.

Raven had never been to the Bahamas, and she knew it would be a good place for her to lay low and recuperate from the stress she had. Raven planned to take advantage of the soothing tropical waters and watch the sun melt away into the sea with a kaleidoscope of color. Raven would enjoy the miles of unspoiled beach that was a world away from the hectic streets of downtown Nassau.

Raven only linked up with Ali six days ago, but she couldn't stop her feelings from running deep. She tried to stop them because Ali was a fugitive, and his chances of getting bagged or killed were high. Raven didn't want to set herself up, but a few days and nights of fucking had her falling in love.

Ali said his friend's wife was expecting her. Raven was nervous and didn't know her. It was better than being interrogated. Raven couldn't thank the owner of the beach house enough.

Raven rang the doorbell twice before she heard shuffling noises behind the door. She didn't know what to expect. When Sonya finally opened the door, Raven's mouth dropped. Raven thought she was seeing a ghost. The women recognized each other and embraced. Sonya remembered Raven vaguely, but well enough to know Raven was the brother of D-Bone, who was killed by the hands of Aaron. Raven recognized Sonya from the times she visited her grandmother and from the picture she found in Aaron's junk drawer. Sonya led Raven into the beach house and got her comfortable.

...

"I met him at a party hosted by one of the biggest drug dealers in California. He seemed nice. I was looking for a come-up so I met him at the right time. We clicked, got deep, and he got me pregnant," Raven said.

Sonya poured herself and Raven a glass of Roscato before sitting next to Raven.

"That's when I found out he killed my brother." Raven was teary eyed, and it pained her to revisit her brother's demise. It disgusted Raven that she slept with her brother's killer, but it wasn't intentional. She felt comfortable with Sonya and trusted her, but not enough to tell her how she and the rest conspired to kill Aaron.

Sonya listened to her attentively as Raven recalled the old picture of Sonya she found in Aaron's junk drawer.

Raven continued, "I tried my hardest to contact you. I called the hospital to see if they could provide your info, but they weren't able to provide that. I was sure he was on his way to Texas to kill you. Thank God he didn't succeed."

Sonya wiped her eyes to limit her own crying. It had been two years since Aaron's attempted murder and rape. Her PTSD was at its peak.

"He almost did. I was out of commission, knocked out from being pistol whipped. When I woke up in the hospital, my sister and brother in law told me how my husband broke out of his restraint, untied everyone, and gave Aaron the ass whipping of his life. They turned the tables on him. When they threw him down the stairs, he vanished," Sonya said.

Sonya and Raven stayed up when the family went to sleep. The women got to know one another and Sonya was grateful for the company. She was stressed out. Lately, her nightmares were high definition. Claude was killed in all of her bad dreams. She spoke to him a few days ago, but the conversation was brief. It didn't matter to Sonya. Hearing Claude's voice soothed her pain. She missed him.

Sahara and Fatima were still at odds, but it subsided a bit because their tension was replaced by the concern of Claude's safety. Destiny started asking questions. She was more in tuned to what was going on than Sahara thought. She was running out of excuses to tell her daughter.

It was a task reading Mark. His body language didn't reveal anything. Sonya had a feeling he knew Claude's movement more extensively; Sonya wasn't going to press him. There was no need to because Mark's lips were sealed.

## 42

## Miami

Thunder, lightening, and an inferno downpour made Calvin's mood more deadly. His pride was at an all time low. Since getting off the jet with Salazar and Zane, his anxiousness and desire to wrap his beefy hands around his wife's petite neck drove him to the brink of intolerable mental pain. Jessica's betrayal rented nothing but space in his mind. The fact that Claude held his only daughter over his shoulder made him nauseous.

Calvin stared at Zane coldly and knew she wore a smile underneath the black pillowcase Salazar covered her head with. If he wanted his daughter to breath another day, he had to resist the urge to shoot her.

Salazar sat next to her with his gun on his hip and his lips pursed. He could only imagine how Calvin felt. He could do nothing but pour Calvin neat cups of Hennessy.

Calvin was so antsy that he wanted to kick his limo driver out the driver's seat and take over the wheel. The only good thing in his case was that Claude could have staged it, but the thought went out the window when he thought of his own grotesque face and body. Juan was a nice looking Hispanic that had the look of a model. Calvin vowed that he would ruin his good-looking ass with a bullet.

Calvin swallowed the rest of his drink when the limo took a right turn and was only minutes away from his residence. As the limo driver got closer, Calvin and Salazar didn't notice anything unusual. They didn't even see a car in the driveway or in front of the swank dwelling. The ringing of his cell phone shattered his deadly thoughts. It was the imposter.

"I see you have the mind of a king; I respect that. Kings would have their inferiors taste food before the king ate. They called them tasters. You threw a few of your men at us while you were in transit. I told you not to do that. Well, your men tasted these bullets. Now it's three dead niggas in your crib stinking the place up. You need proof?" Claude asked.

Calvin still wasn't convinced. He decided to try his luck.

"Prove it," Calvin said icily.

As soon as the words left Calvin's mouth, he heard the limo driver grunt, but he didn't hear the bullet shatter the limo driver's brain.

"Dominic? Dominic!" Calvin yelled.

Calvin nodded at Salazar as to give him the

permission to smash the partition. When he did, Dominic's dead body leaked blood and brain matter all over the front seat.

"Look Calvin, we don't want to murder anymore motherfuckers. Lets keep this short, sweet, and simple. We're watching your every move. The minute you try calling for help, there will be more headshots," Claude warned.

Calvin knew they were using silencers. The rain was so heavy that he doubted anyone heard the shattered glass. He blew a sigh and beckoned Salazar to stash his phone. Calvin looked at the surroundings and had no idea where the shooter's vantage point was located.

"Leave the guns in the limo. When you step out, keep those hands where I could see them. Any funny shit you pull, we shootin' niggas. Got it?" Calvin gritted his teeth. His pride hit rock bottom, but he had no choice but to comply.

"Got it," Calvin said. It took all of his strength to utter those two words.

The front door of the house was left ajar. Calvin and Salazar felt vulnerable without their guns. When they entered, Claude and Ali pulled them in at gunpoint and closed the door.

...

Frightened, sweaty, and fearful for their lives, Jessica and Juan were hogtied together. Juan still had on Calvin's bathrobe, and Jessica was still as naked as the day she was born. Claude finally got Zane on his side again, and Jessica and Juan were at Calvin's disposal. Sayo was safe, sound, and asleep. Not taking any chances, Ali had the gun trained on Calvin and Salazar. Despite a gun being pointed at them, the men were unmoved.

Calvin broke the thick ice.

"You steal my money and take my wife and daughter for ransom. You fucking cocksucker."

Claude smirked.

"You don't own any money Cal, and you damn sure don't own this bitch. You see how shit pop off when your not around?" Claude asked. On cue, Ali played the recording on the phone of Jessica and Juan's sexual noises and the talk of killing Calvin for his life insurance policy. Calvin heard every piece of betrayal. He became so distraught and irritated that he demanded Ali to stop playing it.

"I take orders from no one cuz," Ali said.

Jessica and Juan shivered with fear; it dripped all over their bodies. Despite the adultery and plot, she still didn't want to believe that her husband was capable of killing her. Juan never witnessed Calvin's murderous gaze because he kept his head down. Calvin forcefully snatched his robe off of Juan's body.

"You ungrateful spic! I pull you and your family out of the gutter, and this is how you repay me?" Calvin was so heated that spittle formed in the corners of his mouth.

Juan started crying. He knew he wasn't going to see past tomorrow. He sobbed and choked up. He had no idea how dangerous fucking Jessica was until now.

"Spare my family papi. They had nothing to do with this," Juan begged.

Calvin looked at Juan long and hard. He kept his eyes on Juan while he fished and pulled a knife out of his breast pocket. Without giving it another thought, he stabbed Juan in his Adam's apple and twisted the knife in his gullet. Jessica's posture went limp. She never saw that side of her husband. Jessica hyperventilated and vomited all over herself as Juan's blood spilled onto her. Jessica's attempt to scream was halted by the threat of Ali's gun, which he trained at her. Jessica felt Juan's body twitch a few times before he expired. The scene was so grotesque that Zane turned away.

"You do all this shit for some dyke bitch that ain't giving you no pussy. That's ok though. Tommy and Rocks is in their graves. Your mom is about to catch death at the halfway house she's in," Calvin said gravely.

Calvin gave Claude time to let the threat sink in, but the time was disturbed by two gunshots outside. Calvin knew what it was because he sent off the text a minute before the limo driver got popped. Calvin saw Claude's distraction and tried to rush him, but Ali stepped in and pistol-whipped him. Ali handed Claude the gun out of respect. Calvin looked up at Claude from the floor with no sign of fear.

"I ain't beggin' motherfucker! Get it the fuck on!" Calvin said harshly.

"My mom could take care of herself," Claude said before blowing Calvin's brains out of his head. Calvin's evil, warped mind was all over his suit. Calvin's body was sprawled out across his own living room spewing out blood from the gaping hole in his head.

Jessica screamed loudly. Claude redirected the gun in her direction; the fearful look in her eye made him think twice. Ali didn't have the same reservations. He pulled out the other gun he had stashed and shot her twice in the stomach. Salazar tried to run, but Ali shot him in the back. Salazar wasn't dead. Salazar used the strength in his arms and tried to drag himself away from the shooters. Zane snatched the gun from Ali, walked up to Salazar, and held the gun over his face.

Salazar pleaded, "Amiga...it....it wasn't personal....its how I live..."

"And this is how you die," Zane said before emptying the rest of the clip on him. The heavy rain outside wasn't enough to muffle the noise from the gun. She stood over her first kill holding anger but no regret. Claude snatched her out of her moment along with Ali's desperate plea to get the fuck out of there. The baby crying upstairs didn't deter anyone from leaving. When the police force arrives, they would find the bodies along with a screaming toddler.

Ali felt a sting from the past while in motion en route to the car. He remembered the arguments, fightings, love making, funny moments, sad moments, and the night he found Simone's slain body leaking blood all over the bed with his son present and crying wildly. He thought about holding Simone's hand while she gave birth to his only child

A bullet destroyed that thought. Ali's movement

ceased. Zane prevented him from falling. The visibility in the heavy rain made it next to impossible for Claude to spot the shooter, but he knew gunfire was coming from behind a black Cadillac truck. A third shot exploded from the shooter's cannon. The bullet was so close that Claude heard it whiz by his ear. Zane dragged Ali while Claude took cover and opened fire. He shot blindly in the direction until they made it to the car. The fourth gunshot shattered the back window. The action was so swift that Claude never registered and prepared on the next surprise. His friend Lester.

Lester was slumped over in the front seat of the car with two gaping holes in his head. The weapon Lester used to kill the limo driver was gone. Zane fired Ali's gun nonstop while Claude stood in a trance in deep agony of his friend's murder, but he snapped out of it quick and started shooting.

"Motherfucka!!!" Claude yelled and moved forward as if his body was bulletproof. The shooter ran out of bullets. While the assailant reloaded, Claude took advantage and executed great aim at his head, fired, and caught the shooter in his neck. Zane remained with Ali while Claude checked the scene. The shooter was shot, sprawled out with his hands and legs spread apart, and dead. Claude frisked the man. He snatched the keys the shooter took from Lester's corpse, as well as the gun, and confiscated more weaponry.

After Claude and Zane situated Ali in the car, they pulled off without noticing a second vehicle closing in. Cops swarmed the area seconds after fleeing the vicinity.

# 43

## Miami

Ali rambled things about his son, Simone, and Wade. He claimed that he could see them. His speech became slow, slurred, and sporadic as his life started to fade. Ali saw an angelic Simone smiling warmly at him. She was welcoming him with open arms. Deep in the core of his mind, even with death closing in, Ali embraced it. Without the bullet lodged in his stomach, his fugitive lifestyle would be a total wash.

Ali's eyes were distant. His groans became more intense as he clutched his bleeding and wounded stomach. Blood gushed freely from it. Zane ripped part of her t-shirt, and created a makeshift compress to clot the bleeding.

Claude coasted on the Miami streets with no idea on where to go. He eliminated the shooter but thought there could be more. His next move was dumping the rental and getting a new vehicle. Visuals of Lester's person and remembrance of his advice replayed in his mind. Claude felt responsible, but he knew Lester would rather catch a bullet than being in hospice. His new friend Ali being shot added more insult to injury. The two related on every level known to man. Claude honestly didn't know what to do. If he dropped Ali off at the hospital and Ali survived, he would go to jail for any murder he committed. If he didn't, Ali would surely die. His mind spun as his eyes scanned for any sign on the highway.

"C, pull over," Zane said quietly.

Claude said, "I can't Zane. Niggas could be on to us."

"We have to dump him. It's a few hours to daylight," Zane said quietly. Claude looked in the rearview mirror and looked at Zane coldly.

Claude said, "Are you fucking serious? That motherfucker risked his life for you, and he doesn't know you from a hole in the wall. Fuck you mean dump him?"

"He's dead."

Claude pumped the brake and almost smashed the vehicle into a rig. The shock of his death prevented Claude from seeing the set of headlights closing in on him. Bullets pulled Claude out of his grievance. Zane ducked and took cover. Claude glanced in the rearview mirror and saw the gunman leaning out the window, and aiming a shotgun at the tires. The man fired off a shot and took Claude's tires from him. Claude crashed into a tree off the turnpike. The impact was so intense that Ali's corpse was ejected from the car.

Two masked men pulled Claude and Zane out the car, and they roped them immediately. Once the men covered Claude and Zane's heads with black pillowcases, the mystery men threw them both in the van. The driver pulled off north of the deserted turnpike.

...

Hours after capturing Calvin's killers, Willis, a short dark-skinned drug dealer, and Rick, a light-skinned killer, pulled over to change a flat tire on a gravel road. They were in a wide open country where grass grew on the road's shoulder. Rick could smell the rotten decay of roadkill. They were still in Florida, but a long way from Miami.

Rick leaned against the car, and watched Willis expertly change the tire. Rick was nervous. Two bound people were in the back of the van, and a flat tire could lead to handcuffs. Rick hated taking chances. He was a murderous, illegal immigrant, and his family in Haiti would not be able to eat if he were out of commission. It was daylight, and Willis conversed while he placed the finishing touches of the tire. Willis seemed unmoved by their predicament.

"Ain't nobody got time to grieve for that fat nigga. The motherfucker wouldn't grieve if someone killed us, so the fuck with him. I just want his spot. Other dudes want it, but I want it more," Willis said as he tightened the last lug nut on the van.

Rick said, "You taking your time with that shit. Its not like we are going to work. Lets take these niggas to the spot and cap 'em, plain and simple."

Willis opened the back of the van. Claude and Zane were tied and gagged like animals. After placing the tools back, Willis ignored the sight of them, and he shut the back door of the van.

"Lionel said not to kill them until after he see Claude. That fucker won't be here for hours though, so I hope you have your phone. We should be at the spot in forty minutes," Willis said as Rick sighed in response.

The men got into the van. Willis started it, and he made his way down the gravel road. Rick knew Willis was right. Rick wanted that money. Being ordered to kill two hogtied people was like working for free. It was easy money. Rick lit a cigarette before speaking.

"Lionel is one cocky bastard. Why the fuck does he need to see him?"

Willis adjusted the rearview mirror.

"Because he want to meet the nigga that ended

Calvin. Lionel told that ugly fat motherfucker to leave him alone and take it on the chin. Now Calvin's body is on the slab in the morgue. Stupid prideful fuck," Willis said coldly.

Rick chuckled.

"Did you know Juan was fucking his wife?" Rick asked.

"Yup, and I told Juan he was playing with fire. Now he's dead," Willis said.

As the men conversed, Claude's mind was scrambling on finding a solution. He knew he could take the two goons if given the opportunity. Claude recalled the last time he was bound and hogtied, but that was two years ago, and the restraint Aaron placed him in wasn't that tight. Claude and Zane nodded towards one another as if they were thinking the same thing after hearing the goon's conversation; they had little time. The chances of survival was grim, but Claude didn't give a fuck about odds.

## 44

## Somewhere in Florida

Willis and Rick punched and kicked Claude and Zane viciously while they were hogtied and gagged. The pain Claude experienced in his ribs was excruciating. Zane passed out from the horrific blows. Claude was so disoriented from the hard shots he received that he thought Zane was dead. Now they were both semi-conscious.

While Rick was out getting cigarettes, Willis was having a case of street dreams. With Calvin out of the picture, a takeover was possible, and within reach. Willis placed a smile on his face as the daydream unfolded itself in his head. He was tempted to say thank you to the two fuck bags that put Calvin to sleep. Instead of maintaining close watch on the hostages, he pulled out his phone and hopped on *Facebook*. Willis took a selfie and posted it. It would be a matter of time before Calvin's advisor Lionel arrived.

Willis woke up from a light nap. Five minutes passed since he commented on social media. He checked in on the hostages, and they both were in their places. The sound of a vehicle pulling up in the unpaved driveway grabbed his attention. Willis pulled the dingy brown curtain aside. He saw Lionel getting out of the car. The man was a tall, dreaded, brown skin aging man that had a thin build. Lionel walked slowly up the short flight of stairs and let himself in. Willis nodded at Lionel, but he didn't reciprocate the small social cue as Lionel walked into the room occupied by the hostages. Lionel looked at them and cracked a smirk. He secretly respected Claude. He had to admit it. Lionel knew of Claude just as much as Calvin did. Claude's come up was based off of Calvin's scraps, and Claude had the heart and grit to pull it off.

Claude was on the floor next to Zane bounded and gagged. Lionel knelt down next to him, yanked the cloth out of his mouth, and whispered.

"You got a lot of balls nigga. You murdered a few of Calvin's muscle to rescue this bitch, but too bad you fell short. She must got some dynamite dyke pussy." Lionel shook his head.

Claude grinned.

"We didn't fall short motherfucker. We did exactly what we planned to do."

The man had a death wish. Claude's face was heavily bearded, wild, and unkempt. Claude's eyes looked icily cold. Lionel was going to make sure he acknowledged the man's wish. Zane shot daggers at the guy. The moment Lionel pulled the gun out,

Claude removed his hand from the small of his back, and got a hold of Lionel's wrist, forcing him to drop the gun. Zane sprung from her position on the floor, and she took Lionel's legs from beneath him. Lionel wobbled at first before falling to the floor. Claude picked up the loaded gun. Simultaneously, Willis walked in with his weapon cocked, but Claude moved quicker and fired two shots into his torso. Willis collapsed to the floor, squirmed, grunted, and died. His final moment of agony was etched on his face.

Claude and Zane frisked his pockets, took his money, his loaded Glock 9, and phone. Claude's body was screaming with pain, but his adrenaline outweighed it. It was the second time where he had to undo restraint to save his own life, and those around him courtesy of Mookie, his mother's former and deceased lover who taught him that at a young age. Claude and Zane ran out the front door.

...

Rick pulled up with the van, and he parked behind the black tinted Range Rover. Rick knew it belonged to Lionel. That meant that he was going to inflict death on the hostages and get paid. Rick smiled, but it faded when he saw the two hostages bolt out the front door of the ramshackle abandoned home. Rick and Claude locked eyes briefly. Instinctively, Rick reached for his pistol, but it was too late. Claude sent a volley of bullets Rick's way, shattering the windshield of the van. The bullets struck Rick three times, twice in the chest, and once in the head. A single shard of glass went through his left eye. Rick's body twitched a few times before expiring. Rick still had the lit cigarette wedged in his mouth.

Claude and Zane got into Lionel's Range Rover, and they got the fuck out of dodge.

## 45

## Waterbury

Police officers Chris Dawkins and Reynold Hastings patrolled the inner city, looking for any suspicious activity to kill time. At four in the morning, the city was uneventful, but in a good way. In law enforcement, uneventful was regarded as a great shift. Chris didn't mind it, but his rookie partner hated it. Reynold hated Chris because he was black. Reynold wanted the police force to pair him up with a red neck that twisted rules, or who did a little extra damage to those that didn't want to cooperate with authority. The men had been partners for almost a year. The pair constantly clashed, especially over Reynold's political views. Chris knew that Reynold was a racist based on his subtle remarks and actions. Reynold was a short, stout man in his late twenties who resembled a young Jackie Gleason. Chris was a light skinned middle-aged bald man with deep set eyes. Chris was quiet and tough; he was well respected. Reynold could have cared less about him.

Reynold said, "Donald Trump is just what America needs to rid these ghettos of filth and scum, but then again, we probably wouldn't have a fucking job. Praise to the ghettos! Because of those drug dealing fucks, my wife and I are going to buy a house."

Chris sighed and rolled his eyes. It was difficult to ignore the racist bastard.

"White collar crimes are the worst because they affect everyone. People lose their hard earned fortunes because of those type of motherfuckers," Chris said irately.

"Hey, its better than being poisoned by your own people, right? You people claim police brutality and hate crimes, but the biggest racists are blacks. Blacks kill other blacks through slinging that poisonous shit, or shooting one another. Yeah, real fuckin' sweet," Reynold said sarcastically.

Chris looked at his young rookie partner long and hard and visualized smacking the mucus out his nose. Reynold read his body language, and kept caution indoors. Both of the men fell silent. When they made a left turn on Chase Avenue, the police dispatcher made a description of a black Cherokee leaving a murder crime scene in Bridgeport. Someone saw it in Waterbury and reported it. Reynold drove the vehicle further up Chase; that's when they both noticed the Cherokee the police dispatcher described. The driver of the suspicious vehicle realized they were being followed, and he fled the scene.

...

Fatboy sat in the backseat of the Jeep stunned and numb. In twenty-four hours, Fatboy murdered his crime partner and witnessed a mass murder. The silence made his mind idle. If caught, Fatboy's life was done. Jupe sat shotgun looking spaced out as Flip drove. Flip conducted himself as a seasoned veteran that killed dozens of people. His lips remained pursed as he drove carefully through Waterbury an hour after dropping Jay off at the halfway house.

"Light that reefer up cuz. Lets take some of the edge off. What's done is done," Flip said nonchalantly.

Jupe was so shook that he contemplated jumping out of the moving vehicle. Fatboy had already rolled the blunt after the double murder. The blunt circulated three times in the jeep before the men noticed a patrol car following them. Flip allowed the cruiser to tail him three blocks before peeling off. Sirens appeared in the rearview mirror in the jeep, causing Flip's two passengers to panic.

"Stay the fuck low! I'm going to lose these pigs!" Flip said.

Fatboy and Jupe did exactly what Flip wanted them to do. The Jeep jerked sharply left and right until it skidded and bolted into a new direction. The high-speed chase went on for two minutes until Flip made an abrupt stop on Wigwam Street. Flip pulled out his pistol, and he marked his two passengers.

"Get the fuck out of the jeep...now!" Flip demanded thickly. Fatboy and Jupe looked baffled.

"Nah bro, we in this shit together. We ain't..." Fat Boy was interrupted by the sound of Flip's cocked pistol.

Fatboy stopped his prideful speech when Flip cocked his pistol.

"Either that, or I'll add two more bodies to my resume. Now get the fuck out before I spill some blood!" Flip threatened.

The faint sounds of sirens brought Fatboy back in reality. Jupe was already out of the Jeep, and he walked briskly in the opposite direction. Fatboy aborted the jeep. Without even an informal goodbye, Flip took off into the early morning darkness.

...

"I fuckin' had him! Fuck! I should have just clipped the bastard. Now we fucking lost him," Reynold said as his partner called in other officers. Reynold ran his mouth. Chris shook his head at Reynold's stupidity and wished that he had the wheel. If the redneck weren't a fearful shitty driver, the assailant would have been apprehended. Chris and Reynold cruised around Chase Ave for a few more minutes. Reynold took a right up Hill Street, drove quickly up the steep hill, and spotted the Jeep Cherokee whiz off of Greenwood Ave with a cruiser closing in on his ass. Reynold turned the sirens on, and they joined in on the chase.

...

Flip looked in his rearview mirror and grinned at the pursuing police. He recalled all the events in his natural life, but held no regret. He thought about his ramshackle environment, murders he conducted, deceased family and friends, prison walls, floors, and gates. Flip's future was bleak, and he wanted no part of it. Flip's laughter was filled with insanity as he weaved his way through local traffic with precision. He knew the pigs didn't expect a high-speed chase, but Flip didn't give a fuck. He was a fugitive from justice.

...

Chris grew irate and impatient with Reynold's driving. Reynold would talk that shit about NASCAR potential and aspirations at the station, yet he was driving like he was scared and inexperienced. Chris knew Reynold was full of shit the second he opened his mouth. Luckily, the suspect crashed into a bystander's Volvo.

...

Flip heard all of their demands about getting out of the Jeep, but he moved at his own pace. Flip reached and gripped his loaded pistol, opened the vehicle door, fired two shots, and was riddled with a volley of bullets to his head, neck, and torso. Flip's body looked like it was being electrocuted. Police lit him up badly. Smoke seeped from Flip's fresh wounds.

...

Five officers surrounded Reynold, and Chris was one of them. Reynold's body jerked from the two gaping bullet wounds to his stomach. Blood spilled from his wounds and his mouth. A few officers tried to aide him, but Chris knew it was a lost cause. Chris hated Reynold and at one time, wished bodily harm on him. Chris's memory did not have any remembrance of laughter, camaraderie, and friendship, but Chris was thankful Reynold stood in front of him. Chris's name would have been on those slugs that ripped through Reynold's racist flesh.

## 46

## Greenwich

## Two weeks later

Claude walked himself into an unlocked
mansion, his gun drawn. He took in his surroundings
and was fascinated. Abstract and oil stain paintings
hugged the walls. There was a trio of sofas and
sectionals on top of a cashmere carpet. Claude
proceeded cautiously through the residence, and into
the kitchen. The cabinetry was high end. The gold pot
racks were an average workers one-year salary.

There was a wall of windows framing the six
acres of woods in the backyard. The rectilinear pool in
the back was intended for private use. After leaving the
kitchen, Claude crept up the plush spiral steps. The
barrel of Claude's gun swept everything in his sight.
When he reached the master bedroom, the door was
open. *Someone is in there,* Claude thought. Claude
could see feet at the base of the cantilevered oak bed.
He walked slowly in the room with his gun trained
thinking the job was a lot easier than he thought.
When Claude saw whom he was supposed to kill, he
recoiled in shock. Someone beat Claude to the target.
The pillow next to the body had a hole in it. Percy's
eyes were opened, and the gaping hole in his head was

fresh. The naked, doughy woman next to him suffered the same fate.

Claude's senses were heightened. There was no smell of decomposition, but he smelled insect repellent on the bodies. He didn't know how long the bodies been there. Claude raised his weapon and made moves. He thought about security and knew there had to be cameras in the house. Claude knew police might be on their way. He couldn't leave until the security system was destroyed. Claude checked most of the rooms until he found it. Someone beat him to that as well. The security system was smashed.

Claude retraced his steps back to the bodies. He needed to find their cell phones to disable any app pertaining to a security system. Luckily, Percy and Sherry didn't have them. Sherry did, however, have twenty missed calls from her friend Heather. Instead of exploring the mansion, Claude vanished. Heather would check up on Sherry, run into two dead surprises, and call the police.

Percy and Sherry lay naked and dead because of Percy's past. Sherry was nothing more than collateral damage. Percy was living on borrowed time the second he lost the Dominican's kilos. Ali couldn't touch him, and Claude was too late. Karma would kill anyone who lived a life of filth.

## Epilogue

Former Detective Taft submitted his retirement papers the prior week. Today, he packed all his shit from his office into a few boxes, and hauled it to his car. He spent the majority of his life solving cases and less time on his marriage. Taft did what he had to do to break open the Peter Sullivan case, and now it was solved based on Walter Banks' testimony. Taft didn't know how viable Flex's testimony was, but he didn't give a shit. Taft was tired, and he was done.

After putting the last box in the trunk, Taft drove off, and he didn't give the station a last glance. It was time for him to enjoy his life.

...

Flex sat on his bunk against the wall while silently rejoicing the day he had. He received a visit from his grandparents and mother, got some cash from Octavia, and heard that Ali and Flip were plant food. Octavia's input and his own instinct served him correct. Flex told authority that Ali and Flip were probably in New York with Raven, and he admitted that he watched Aaron shoot Peter. Flex knew the legal system wouldn't give him credit for Ali and Flip because Ali was killed in Florida, Flip was gunned down in Connecticut, and Raven was still missing.

They were all worthless in the eyes of society. It was all about the Peter Sullivan case. Flex's grandparents took home and locked up the copy of his *proffer agreement* just in case his lawyer reported fuckery from the judge. Flex still had a lot of time to serve. A decade in prison was better than twenty-five to life. Today was indeed a good day for Flex.

...

The apartment had been quiet since Sylvia took the baby to Philadelphia for the weekend. It was perfect timing. Fat Boy was paranoid and cagey since he killed his crime partner and witnessed Flip inflict a mass murder in Bridgeport. Fat Boy saw Calvin's demise on the news two weeks ago, along with his wife, and a few of his muscle. For two weeks, Fat Boy felt like a sucker. He felt Claude left him with a shitty conscious, and no money and future. Fat Boy wanted to put a bullet in Claude for deceiving him, but he took it back. Fat Boy received a mysterious phone call an hour ago. Now Fat Boy was in front of the man that he wanted to kill. Claude didn't get into too much detail about what took place in Florida. Claude left Fat Boy with beyond an educated guess on what happened. Claude succeeded on getting Zane back. Fat Boy had a feeling Ali and Lester didn't have much luck on the suicide mission. He damn sure wasn't going to question Claude about it. The war on Claude's body told all.

Fat Boy was looking at an open army-sized duffle bag holding forty, ten-thousand dollar stacks on his kitchen table. Claude pulled out twenty stacks, and left the other twenty in the duffle bag. Fat Boy was speechless. Claude used the silence as his cue to inform him of his final plan.

"You can have the rest bro. If you don't want to take anymore risks, you can take twenty stacks and slide, or you can take it all," Claude said.

Fat Boy wanted to take the money and slide, but his gambling mindset shifted him in a different direction.

Fat Boy asked, "What do I need to do to earn that?"

Claude patted Fat Boy on the shoulder. "Listen carefully." Claude ran him the final plan. After hearing it, Fat Boy deemed the plan easy money.

...

Police officer Chris Dawkins arrived by himself to a homicide scene at the intersection of East Main Street and Meriden Road at three o'clock in the morning. It was his first day back after two weeks.

Chris was grateful to be alive. His near death experience was traumatic for him, and he could have taken more time, but Chris didn't want to. He wanted and needed to work. Two weeks ago, after relentlessly pursuing a homicide suspect, the gunman calmly got out of the car, and fired two shots before police cut the gunman down with bullets. If Chris's racist partner Reynolds wasn't standing in front of him, Chris would have been the one being lowered into the ground with military honors.

Chris walked through a labyrinth of police, crime scene investigators, and news reporters. Taylor, a tall lean Italian man with a receding hairline in his late thirties, and Chris's best friend on the police force, beckoned him to come closer. When Chris made his way over, Taylor lifted the crime scene tape for Chris's entry. Chris got a clear view of the body. The victim didn't look familiar, but Taylor had worked the police force in Bridgeport before being transferred to the Waterbury Police Department, and knew the victim had a lengthy police record.

"Two weeks got you lazy man. It's about time you arrived. We are about to wrap this shit up," Taylor said jokingly.

Chris watched the coroner's transporters load

the body inside the coroner's van. He asked, "Who is the vic?"

"Jaheim Beck. On the streets, they call him Jay. He was one of Bridgeport's finest informants. Put a lot of people away. No one will be losing sleep over this fucker. He was in and out of prison since he was thirteen. Burned a lot of people and bridges," Taylor said.

"Any leads?" Chris asked.

"Nothing. Not a single witness. And get this; his address is the halfway house up the street. He was due for discharge tomorrow," Taylor said.

"Wow. Criminals are going to rejoice. This is the price a person pays when they play dirty," Chris said.

Taylor said, "You can say that again. Breakfast on you this morning?"

"Yes, breakfast is on me you cheap bastard," Chris quipped before both officers shared a laugh and went their separate ways.

. . .

Claude rode in the backseat of a taxi in Coral Harbour. The catastrophe in his timeline was huge. Tears spilled down his face as he thought about his people. Claude lost Lester, Flip, Rocks, Tommy, Tank, and had just parted ways with Zane at the airport. As the cab driver merged off the highway, Claude thought about how valuable Jay's information was. Jay's information was the reason why Zane was still breathing, but it was too bad Claude had Jay slain. Claude had been locked up too long to not smell a rat. The extra two hundred thousand dollars Claude gave Fat Boy to gun Jay down was worth it.

...

Raven read an article titled "A Small World," and it centered on Peter Sullivan, and the unknown name that connected the dots of the crime spree. It was dug out of a cold case file that contained many names. When the article got deeper, Raven knew who connected the dots. The article started with Colin, Earl, B-Bum, and her brother D.Bone's demise. Tears spilled down Raven's face as she recalled the last time she seen her brother alive. Hatred filled Raven's soul when she thought about her brother's killer.

Before Raven read the article, Sonya explained to Raven in detail of how jealous Aaron was of D. Bone before the mass murders took place. Raven knew the rest. Raven knew Ali, Flip, and Wade set up Marco, Scoot, and Jimmy for a massacre, and succeeded even though their attackers were gunned down at the same moment. Besides Aaron killing Peter, Raven also found out why she had a hard time getting in touch with Ali. Ali and Flip were killed on the same day nearly three weeks ago under different circumstances on the same night. The article connected Ali and Flip as cousins. Raven's anxiety increased when she saw her own name in the article. The author of the article stated that Raven wanted vengeance. She was the reason why there was war on the streets, and that her whereabouts remain a mystery. When Raven was done reading the article, a taxi pulled up directly in front of her. When the man stepped out of it, Raven knew who he was at first glance. She knew Sonya and the rest of the family were expecting him. She gave Claude that respect, but at some point, she needed closure.

...

Claude was relaxed, got reacquainted with his family, and was settling back into civilian lifestyle. It had been two days since he arrived at Coral Harbour. Tragic trends seem to be the theme of his life. Claude hoped he completed his last mission. Despite Claude's adversaries dead and buried, he wasn't going to put his guard down. A man like Calvin had goons all over the world. And Claude would cut each and everyone of them down if anyone poses as a threat to him and his family.

Claude knew the people involved in his mission had a death wish, but the thought of losing everyone drove him to the brink of insanity. Still, there was hope for him. Sonya was Claude's reminder that he wasn't alone, and he valued that.

Claude and Sonya relaxed under a beach umbrella cuddling while everyone went swimming. It was their last day in hiding. Sonya stood and went to go get her feet wet in the ocean. Claude stole a glance as she smiled radiantly. Sonya seemed complete and colorful since Claude arrived. He loved every inch of her. Raven stepped into his line of sight, obstructed his view of his wife, and cut straight to the chase.

Raven said, "I don't need much from you Claude. I just want to hear some more detail. Did Ali suffer?"

Her question placed Claude in a dark place. He could still hear the cacophony of bullets and Ali's groaning after being shot. Claude couldn't shake the thoughts. He preferred to never talk about it again, but Raven was an exception; he had a message for her.

Claude said, "A little. We were getting shot at. The gunman missed me and Zane, but Ali got popped in the chest while we ran. We managed to get him in the car and pull off. A mile later, he was dead." Raven had a right to know, but Claude wasn't in the mood to be questioned.

Even though Raven knew some detail about it, Claude's revelation stunned her. Tears flowed gently down her face. Claude gave her a moment to gather herself. Hearing that about the man that romanced her and killed for Raven stung. When she stopped crying, Raven took a good look at the healing scar Claude had on his forehead.

"I'm confused Claude. Ali was found dead by himself off the highway with gun shot wounds two hundred feet away from a bullet-riddled car in Florida. There were no witnesses, explanations, nothing. The wounds he had on his face would have disfigured Ali for life. And his cousin Flip was killed by police in Connecticut the very same day. Where were you and your friend Zane? I sure hope she was worth it," Raven said with a hint of disdain.

If Claude were ten years younger, he would have given the bitch the verbal onslaught for coming at him like that. Raven didn't know shit and her approach went south. An article depicted Raven as a possible conspirator to multiple homicides, and Raven was judging Claude? This tested his patience. Claude understood Raven's anger, and decided to give her the benefit of the doubt. Claude was quiet. He needed the time to process what she said even though it wasn't necessary.

Claude said, "Zane was worth it Raven. I would have done that for you if you were in her shoes, and we are real like that. For you to tell me that me and Zane stood on the sideline while everyone fought and got killed, that's a smack in the face. I have to live with that shit everyday, not you." Claude's anger was beginning to boil, but he had it under control.

"So what was the price for Ali and Flip dying for you?" Raven asked

Claude looked at her like she lost her mind.

"Percy."

Percy's name zapped the breath out of her. Hearing Percy's name felt foreign coming out of Claude's mouth. Raven thought twice about talking that slick shit again. She humbled herself. Guilt invaded the rest of the space in her head. If Raven didn't wish Percy dead, Ali would still be alive.

Claude took his shades off and faced her.

"I've known Flip for fifteen years, and he was one of the realist dudes I knew. I did my entire bid with him, and I knew he wasn't built for society. It hit me when I heard the cops shot him. I put things in perspective and I realize that I am more at peace with him being dead," Claude said.

Raven gave him an incredulous look.

"I don't understand the rationale of that statement," Raven said politely.

"Nothing to understand. I have fifteen years worth of friendship and conversation with the man, and he was a man of his word," Claude said before continuing. "Flip told niggas to get out of the car minutes before being gunned down. He didn't want anyone participating in his demise. He told me on the last day of my bid that he would kill himself before going back to jail. He meant that shit. And he even took out a cop." Claude took out a freshly rolled blunt and lit it. "And that's how I'm putting it in perspective. And you should do the same. Ali was tired Raven. At the rate he was going, he would have been dead or locked up by the end of the year. He knew he would never see his son again, and that shit ate him like a disease. If he couldn't be around his son, then he had no reason to live and you know that."

Raven was quiet. Claude was right, but putting it in perspective was a lot easier said than done, she thought. Raven felt vindicated though. Hearing about Percy's death brought her satisfaction and justice.

Raven asked, "So how did…?"

"I didn't," Claude interjected. "Somebody beat me to it. Him and his fat white chick got murdered together."

*Dominicans,* Raven thought.

Raven said, "Ali helped you and you were going to put Percy down…favor for a favor."

Claude nodded.

"Exactly. I was going to put him down. Ali, Flip, and Lester gave their lives so I can have this conversation, so yeah, even in death, I was about to make that happen," Claude said.

Claude reached in his book bag and pulled out a generic looking smartphone. He scrolled until he reached the gallery. After Claude found what he was looking for, he handed Raven the phone. Raven stared at Percy and Sherry's dead bodies for thirty seconds before handing the phone back to him. Claude chucked the phone into the ocean from his position on the beach chair.

Raven said, "I'm sorry I offended you. You did me a favor having me come down here, and I don't know where I mustered up the nerve to pop shit."

Claude decided not to invest too much into her reckless question and statement. It pissed him off a little, but he understood.

"No worries. Listen, Ali told me that if anything happened to him, he wanted me to help you. I'm going to honor that. If you have a little money, you can stay here, and maintain the place until you are ready to resurface," Claude proposed.

Raven smiled and sighed.

"If that ever happens," Raven said.

Claude said, "Listen, every motherfucker in that article is dead. Even if they reel you in for questioning, there is no concrete proof that you orchestrated that shit. There is not even enough proof for an arrest... unless y'all was discussing murder related shit through text on a Verizon plan."

Raven smiled at his sarcasm.

"And besides, from what I got out of the article, they were mainly interested in that white boy," Claude continued. "They ain't thinking about no gang bangers or drug dealers. It was all about those grieving white parents who wanted closure for their son. Case closed. If it makes you feel better, kick it here as long as you want. Real talk. If you got bread to support yourself, you good."

"I appreciate this Claude. I still feel like a bitch for snapping at you. If you need me to do anything for you, you know where I'm at. I will earn my way," Raven said confidently.

"Definitely." Claude stood up to greet his incoming family with Sonya leading the way. The tension between everyone was uplifted. Raven stood up and joined them; it was the start of a possible new life for her.

...

Zane moved to a ocean house apartment home in San Diego a month after her rescue in an attempt to ditch her troubled past. She arrived with a new name and identity. Zane blended in smoothly with the community. She still, however, preferred to keep to herself. She wasn't in the right state of mind to party, date, or mingle. Zane rarely slept; the sight of Mercedes's face when that bullet took her life haunted her. She stopped smoking weed because it made her too paranoid. The last time Zane smoked, she thought she saw Salazar, the only man she had ever killed.

She watched the sun disappear into the Pacific Ocean from her deck. Zane's mind was swirling with questions about her life. Claude murdered people to rescue her, and Zane began to wonder if it was worth it. She questioned her existence. The depression Zane felt was heavy. She was insulted, assaulted, molested, and covered with shit for a week. Zane felt the psychological effects from her kidnapping.

Zane only spoke to Claude and a handful of people. She had more than enough money to start a new life, but the demons from her past rented space in her mind. Zane had a tough journey ahead of her. Despite the consequences, Zane would never leave her home without her gun.

...

Six months later, after boarding the bus to Bradley International Airport, Delores settled in her seat near the window. She discharged from the halfway house after six months. Delores was end of sentence. Prison was the worst event in her life's timeline. She could still see the agony stretched across Mookie's handsome features after Delores pulled the knife out of his heart seventeen years ago. The look Mookie had on his face looked like the look Chester had on his face when Delores poked holes all over his body outside the club six months ago. Despite leaving Chester's grotesque body in a dark alley, she felt no regret.

Delores smiled when she thought about the good times she shared with Lester in their heyday as youths. She had no idea Claude used to work with him. Lester was the baddest motherfucker in Waterbury at one point. Even in sickness, Lester never lost his touch with the underworld. Delores knew the extent of Lester's criminal grind more than Claude did.

When Delores found out Darlene was entering the rehabilitation side of the halfway house with the monkey still on her back, her anger towards Darlene resurfaced. The more Delores looked at Darlene, the more Delores's anger grew. As the days passed, Patty, a lifer, Delores best friend while incarcerated at York, wrote Delores, and told her that Darlene wanted in on the one hundred thousand dollar reward for Claude's head, and that Patty knew the woman who Darlene approached about the tag. Thanks to Lester and his resources, Delores was able to obtain laced Fentanyl, a needle, and raw and uncut heroin from him because Delores heard Darlene was secretly inquiring about the dope.

On visiting day, a day after she stabbed Chester to death, Delores saw an opportunity. While everyone was outside with their families, including Darlene, Delores put on a pair of plastic gloves, pulled the dope needle out of her pocket, and left the needle of death on Darlene's bed. She left no prints on the syringe.

Delores killed two birds with one stone in one

night while under the watchful eye of Connecticut Department of Correction. When she came home from prison, Delores didn't intend to kill anyone, but people intended to kill her son. Delores harbored no regret.

Three hours later, Delores waited for her luggage at Fort Worth/Dallas International Airport. When she saw Claude, Sahara, Destiny, Mark, and the rest of the extended family, she broke down and cried. Delores felt at home already.